THE HEALING HERESY

A Biblical Examination of The Theology of the Healing Movement

G. Michael Cocoris

© 1999, 2024 by G. Michael Cocoris

All rights reserved. This publication may not be reproduced (in whole or in part, edited, or revised) in any way, form, or means, including, but not limited to electronic, mechanical, photocopying, recording or any kind of storage and retrieval system *for sale*, except for brief quotations in printed reviews, without the written permission of G. Michael Cocoris, 2016 Euclid #20, Santa Monica, CA 90405, michaelcocoris@gmail.com, his appointed representatives. Permission is hereby granted, however, for the reproduction of the whole or parts of the whole without changing the content in any way for *free distribution,* provided all copies contain this copyright notice in its entirety. Permission is also granted to charge for the cost of copying.

Unless otherwise indicated, all Scripture quotations are taken from the New King James Version ®, Copyright © 1979, 1980, 1982 by Thomas Nelson, Inc. Used by permission. All rights reserved.

Cover by Victoria Marshall

Interior layout by John T. ocoris

TABLE OF CONTENTS

Preface

Chapter

1 The Modern Healing Movement   1

2 Is All Sickness From Satan?   19

3 Is It Always God's Will To Heal?   31

3 Did Chist Die For Sickness?   47

5 Does The Gift of Healing Exist Today?   59

6 Does Your Healing Depend On Your Faith?   83

7 Does God Heal Today?   95

8 Conclusion   109

Bibliography   115

About The Author   119

PREFACE

The painful reality of sickness, combined with the admitted limitations of modern medicine, has pushed many to seek divine intervention. The ever-present TV healing evangelist insists that God can and does heal the sick. Thousands flock to see and/or seek healing.

Faith healers claim that what they teach about healing is based on the Bible and that it works. Unfortunately, the experience of many with faith healers has not only caused confusion, it has also resulted in pain and even death. Since they claim biblical authority, the first and foremost issue is, "Is what faith-healers teach biblical?

Not all divine healers agree on every detail of what the Bible teaches about sickness and healing, but there is a "healing theology," which, more or less, characterizes the healing movement.

The dictionary definition of "theology" is "the study of God and the relationship between God and the universe." Calvinism, a theological system that consists of five points, is an illustration. The five points are: 1) Total depravity. 2) Unconditional election. 3) Limited Atonement. 4) Irresistible grace. 5) Perseverance of the Saints. Three of those five points are about God: the Unconditional Election of God the Father, the Limited Atonement of God the Son, and the Irresistible Grace of God the Holy Spirit. The first and last points are about people.

The Healing Heresy

Generally, faith healers within the modern American Protestant healing movement believe and teach five healing theology tenets. The five tenants of the healing movement are: 1) All sickness is of Satan. 2) It is the will of God the Father for all to be healed. 3) Christ died for sickness as He died for sin. 4) The Holy Spirit gives some believers the gift of healing today. 5) The sick person must have faith to be healed. Like the theological system of Calvinism, the theology of the healing movement includes each member of the Trinity and individuals. Unlike the five points of Calvinism, the theological of the healing movement includes Satan.

Is the healing theology biblical? Each point of its theology needs to be examined to answer that question. First, a brief history of the modern healing movement will be considered. Then, the five doctrinal tenets of the healing theology will be examined. This is a theological treatment of the healing theology, but along the way, an accurate, balanced, and clear understanding of the biblical teaching concerning sickness and healing, as well as its practical ramifications, will be pointed out.

Many thanks to Teresa Rogers for her labor of love in reading this and many other manuscripts of mine.

May the Lord use the information presented to provoke those who read it to arrive at a biblical theology of healing.

G. Michael Cocoris
Santa Monica, California

Chapter 1

THE MODERN HEALING MOVEMENT

Faith healers claim that their ministry recaptures the essence of biblical Christianity. They insist they are doing the same thing Christ and the apostles did. Some point to similar movements, which have periodically emerged throughout church history.

Yet, in theology and methodology, the healing movement within Protestant Christianity is a modern phenomenon. When, then, did the modern healing movement begin? The following is a brief history of the healing movement.

A. J. Gordon

The general impression today is that healing is part and parcel of the modern Pentecostal movement, which began shortly after the turn of the twentieth century. The healing movement, however, predates the Pentecostal/charismatic movement.

The doctrinal foundation of the healing movement is the teaching that healing is in the atonement. That doctrine has been called the Magna Carta of the healing theory. In his book *Faith Healing and the Christian Faith*, Wade H. Boggs, Jr., a theology professor, says, "So far as I have been able to discover, the theory that healing for all faithful Christians is in the atonement originated with a well-known Boston theologian and preacher, A. J. Gordon" (Boggs, p. 81). Gordon's book, *The Ministry of Healing*, was published in 1882. Boggs explains that Gordon's language reveals that he regarded the idea of healing in the atonement "as a tentative suggestion, more in the sphere of inquiring and investigation than in the sphere of dogma."

Boggs' assessment is accurate. Gordon wrote: "In the atonement of Christ, there seems to be a foundation laid for faith in bodily healing. Seems—we say, for the passage to which we refer is so profound and unsearchable in its meaning that one would be very careful not to speak dogmatically regarding it. However, it is as at least a deep and suggestive truth that we have Christ set before us as the sickness-bearer as well as the sin-bearer of His people" (Gordon, p. 16).

Gordon quotes Matthew 8:17. "In other words, the passage seems to teach that Christ endured vicariously our diseases as well as our iniquities" (Gordon, p. 17). He also quotes Dr. Hovey's book, *The Miracles of Christ*, which supports his "suggestion." Thus, Gordon was not the first person to offer this idea in print. At any rate, later in his book, Gordon states, "Has the gospel no office of healing and blessing to proclaim meantime for the physical part of man's nature? In answering this question, we only make the following suggestions, which point significantly in one direction" (Gordon, p. 19).

Gordon "suggested" that the church failed to appropriate this truth because of its lack of faith and quotes Bengel to prove it. "The reason why *many* miracles are not now wrought is not so much because faith is established as that unbelief reigns" (Bengel, cited by Gordon, p. 24). After examining Mark 16, Gordon writes,

"We conclude, therefore, that this text teaches that the miraculous gifts were bestowed to abide *in the church* to the end, though not that every believer should be endowed with them" (Gordon, p. 28).

Many, then, of the basic tenants of the healing movement were "suggested" by A. J. Gordon. Those who came after him developed these "suggestions."

G. O. Barns

One of the first faith healers was G. O. Barns. He began his ministry as a missionary to India and later pastored a Presbyterian church in the United States. Because of discouragements with the synod, Barns resigned and, for a short time, developed an interest in the Plymouth Brethren. He then became an assistant to D. L. Moody, who advised him to become an evangelist. The Holiness Church also influenced him.

At first, Barns emphasized only evangelism. Later, he added a healing ministry. Concerning the origin of his healing ministry, he wrote in his diary, "Visited Mr. and Mrs. Cotton. Both are lying in the same bed, suffering from neuralgia. I was so moved by the sight of these dear young people, thus about to be cut off in the midst of their days, that I determined henceforth, in the name of the Lord, to "obey the gospel" and fully carry out my commission not only to preach the gospel but "heal the sick" as the Lord gave power and occasion. The dear Master has been turning my heart in this direction for some time, and in simple reliance on Him alone,

I will do "what in me lies" to rescue the victims of Satan from his awful clutches" (Simson, pp. 28-29).

Because of his healing ministry, many testified of being miraculously cured of such ailments as cancer, nervous conditions, rheumatism, etc. He also had failures. He wrote, "I learned last night the secret of apparent failures in bodily healing. It is just as in the soul—some are just saved from hell, some go on to one degree of advancement, and some to another. In the body, some may be saved from death, who yet are not relieved from aging and suffering, and therefore have received nothing, as the man saved from hell, yet not from temper or drunkenness, seems to have gotten nothing.... I cannot tell how this clear teaching gave comfort in view of so many apparent failures in those who trust the best they can. The degrees are as manifest as in the soul's saving. I believe now the weakest faith saves from death, as the weakness of faith saves the soul from perishing" (Simson, p. 29).

In 1882, Barns met with A. B. Simpson, the Christian and Missionary Alliance founder, and assisted him in one of his consecration and healing meetings.

A. B. SIMPSON

Albert Benjamin Simpson was born at Cavendish, Prince Edward Island, on December 15, 1844. He graduated from Knox College in Toronto in 1865 and pastored the Knox Presbyterian Church in Hamilton, Ontario from 1865 to 1874.

Simpson became the pastor of a church in Louisville, Kentucky.

During this period of his life, he experienced what he described as "the fullness of the blessing of Christ." This concept later became the foundation for his teaching on sanctification.

In 1880, he moved to New York City, where he suffered a severe illness. A physician told him that he did not have enough constitutional strength to last more than a few months. He and his family took some time off at Old Orchard Beach in Maine, where there were meetings at a campground. He later said that up to that time in his life, he had not committed himself in any full sense to the truth or experience of divine healing. However, he had seen a man healed, which impressed him greatly. He had also heard a great number of people testify that they had been healed simply by trusting the Lord. This drove him to his Bible, where he became convinced that healing was part of Christ's gospel. Simpson began speaking of the four-fold gospel: Jesus Christ as Savior, Sanctifier, Healer, and coming King.

In 1884, Simpson wrote his first book, *The Gospel of Healing*. The first three chapters had appeared in 1883 as articles in his magazine, *The Word, the Work, and the World*, and as a series of tracts. In these writings, Simpson taught that healing was in the atonement.

In 1883, Simpson opened a Bible and missionary training school, which later moved to Nyack, New York, on the Hudson River. He organized the Christian Alliance in 1887 and the International Missionary Alliance in 1889. These two organizations were later combined to form the Christian and Missionary Alliance (1897), a group built on the four-fold gospel, which included healing.

The Christian and Missionary Alliance is an active "denomination" today. Like its founder, this group does not major on divine healing. Their emphasis is on evangelism, the Christian life, and world missions. Their practice of healing is not extreme and certainly not flamboyant. However, their pastors anoint with oil and pray for the sick, but they do not sensationalize healing, as do many deliverance evangelists.

According to Harrell, a history professor who wrote a history of the healing movement, A. J. Gordon, the Boston Baptist, and A. B. Simpson, a Presbyterian who became the founder of the Christian and Missionary Alliance Fellowship, were simply pioneer teachers on divine healing. Others were trailblazers, but John Alexander Dowie founded healing revivalism in America.

John Alexander Dowie

John Alexander Dowie was born in Edinburgh, Scotland, on May 25, 1847. At six years of age, he signed a pledge against the use of intoxicating liquors. He was opposed to drinking and smoking all of his life. When John Alexander was thirteen, his parents immigrated to Australia. Years later, he returned to Scotland, where he entered Edinburgh University. After three years at the university, he returned to Australia, where he became a Congregationalist and later a nondenominational pastor.

In 1875, Dowie became the pastor of the Congregational Church in Newtown, a suburb of Sydney. While he was the pastor of that church, a plague swept through Australia that claimed hundreds of lives. Within a few weeks, he officiated at more than forty funerals. Seeing this physical suffering drove him to pray for a message. Based on Acts 10:38, he concluded that Satan was the defiler and Christ was the healer. He exclaimed, "I will never say, 'God's will be done' to Satan's work, which God's own Son came to destroy, and this is one of them" (Lindsay, p. 24). Dowie prayed for several to recover and they did. In fact, from that moment on, not another person in his flock died of the epidemic. Dowie, however, did not begin at once to preach or practice healing.

In 1882, the same year A. J. Gordon published his book on healing in America, Dowie began to preach healing in Australia. In 1883, he determined that he would introduce and regularly practice the ministry of divine healing in his church in Melbourne. He boldly proclaimed the gospel of healing in his own church and in open-air meetings where, on at least one occasion, he preached to an audience of as many as 20,000 people. He also vehemently denounced the liquor industry.

In 1886, he founded the International Divine Healing Association, which soon had a number of branches in various parts of Australia and New Zealand. It is interesting to note that in the same year he received an invitation to attend an international conference on divine healing and true holiness, which was to be held in London, England; Dowie himself was unable to attend the London meeting.

Dowie migrated to America in 1888, ultimately settling in Chicago, Illinois. In 1893, he began conducting services in a small tabernacle. The next year, he started the publication of a weekly periodical called *The Leaves of Healing*. Although it is no longer published weekly, *The Leaves of Healing* is still in circulation. Within a short period, the sick and disabled pursued him in such droves that Dowie leased and furnished several large rooming houses to be used as healing houses.

Dowie taught that the sick should disregard all medical treatment, even for infectious diseases and broken bones. According to him, doctors, drugs, and druggists were all of the devil. When asked about the undeniable failures of faith cures, he replied that no one could be cured without faith and that the sickness stayed, which proved that the patient did not have enough faith. Dowie taught, to one degree or another, all the tenets of what later became the healing theology of the healing movement.

Because of his teaching, several deaths occurred in his homes. In 1895, after an investigation by the authorities, he was charged with, among other things, manslaughter, neglect, and practicing medicine without a license. The higher courts, however, ruled that the city's hospital ordinance, which he was charged with violating, was unconstitutional.

In 1896, Dowie founded the Christian Catholic Church. His dream was to organize a church based on apostolic principles. He did not believe that the days of miracles had passed or that the gifts of the Spirit had been withdrawn. According to him, the prophetic office was to be permanent, as was also the office of apostle. During the formation of the church, when it was suggested that he become an apostle, Dowie said, "I do not think that I have reached a deep enough depth of true humility; I do not think that I have reached a deep enough depth of true abasement and self-effacement, for the high office of apostle, such as he had reached who could say and mean it too, I am least than the least of all the saints and am not worthy to be called an apostle" (Lindsay, p. 155). Concerning the new church, Dowie also said, "In things that are essential, we demand unity. In things that are not essential, we give the fullest liberty, and we must do all things in charity."

Dowie had another vision. He dreamed of building a city where drugs, tobacco, liquor, theaters, brothels, dance halls, and the like would be forever barred. As the clock struck midnight on New Year's Eve, 1900, Dowie, the general overseer of the Christian Catholic Church, pulled a cord, a curtain rolled back from a canvas and revealed a great map, which showed the site of a dream city to be named Zion located forty miles north of Chicago on Lake Michigan. Dowie had managed to secure 6000 acres, a tract of land about ten square miles, in the area north of Waukegan. The plan called for the land not to be sold but leased for 1100 years. The terms of each lease strictly forbid the possession or use of tobacco, liquor, or swine's flesh anywhere within the limits of Zion. No doctor's offices or drugstores were to be located there. No gambling houses, theaters, or dance halls were ever to receive a license to operate in the city of Zion. A temple was to occupy the center of the city. Streets emanated in all directions from the temple.

Dowie's dream was ambitious. Other Zion cities were to be built all over the world, including one at Jerusalem. Ultimately, Jesus Christ Himself would rule from Jerusalem over a world from which all evil, all sickness, all poverty, and all unhappiness would be purged.

Dowie and his followers plunged themselves into the building of Zion. Within two years, ten thousand people had moved to his community. The rule of Zion was to be held firmly and absolutely in the hands of the general overseer. There was no balance of power. Dowie said, "Zion is to be a theocracy, not a democracy." Dowie exercised personal control over the most minor details of the community's existence.

In 1901, Dowie proclaimed himself to be Elijah, the restorer. He not only claimed the fulfillment of the prophecy of the last two verses of the Old Testament, but he also claimed that he was the fulfillment of the prophecy of "the prophet" in Deuteronomy 18:18-19. Furthermore, he declared himself to be the messenger of the covenant as foretold in Malachi 3:1-3. Dowie believed that the ministry of his office and the ministry of his Restoration Host would affect world changes that would ultimately usher in the millennium and the return of Christ. There were other excesses, and before he died, leaders within his movement suspended him from the office of general overseer. On September 24, 1905, Dowie suffered a stroke, which left him paralyzed on his left side. On March 9, 1907, he passed away. Dowie's biographer, Gordon Lindsay, claimed that God raised Dowie up to reintroduce divine healing to the church of Jesus Christ. Undoubtedly, Dowie was the trailblazer for the theology and practice of healing within American Protestant Christianity in the twentieth century.

Zion, Illinois, and the Christian Catholic Church still exist today. Both have undergone a great deal of change over the years. The Christian Catholic Church still believes and practices healing but by no means of the extreme variety. Today, the Christian Catholic Church is very similar to the Christian and Missionary Alliance Church.

CHARLES F. PARHAM

Inspired by Dowie's example, Charles F. Parham opened the Bethel Healing Home in Topeka, Kansas in 1898. In 1900, he founded the Bethel Bible School, where, in 1901, the Pentecostal movement began.

One of his students, William J. Seymour, a black holiness preacher, carried the message of the baptism of the Holy Spirit with the evidence of speaking in tongues to Azusa Street in Los Angeles, California. On April 9, 1906, an integrated group, composed mostly of whites, began to speak in ecstatic utterances. These meetings continued almost without stopping for about three months. During this time, miraculous healings were reported. From Los Angeles, the Pentecostal movement expanded throughout the United States and, by 1908, had spread to other countries. Thus, the Pentecostal movement came out of the healing movement, not vice versa.

F. F. Bosworth

Out of Zion, Illinois, also came F. F. Bosworth and his brother B. B. Bosworth. The Bosworth family moved to Zion when the two boys were young. Fred F. Bosworth served as band director at Dowie's church. About 1910, he moved to Dallas, Texas, where he built a strong, independent church and pastored it for ten years. After World War I, he began conducting revival crusades.

In the 1920s, Bosworth's healing campaigns filled great auditoriums, seating thousands of people. He wrote, "In our last revival preceding the writing of this book conducted in Ottawa, Canada, during the seven weeks of the meetings, six thousand came for healing, and about twelve thousand for salvation. I doubt if there would have been more than one thousand for salvation had it not been for the miracles of healing that displayed the compassion of the Lord. The city and the country were stirred as never before in its history, and the largest crowds that ever gathered under one roof for religious meetings in this capital of Canada filled the newly-built million-dollar auditorium—the largest building in the city. The attendance ran as high as ten thousand in a single service" (Bosworth, p. 71).

Other meetings attracted up to twelve thousand people. One admirer of Bosworth wrote of him, "By the late twenties, the Bosworth revival had electrified dozens of cities in the United States and Canada, and the work of this man had already had a profound impact on an entire generation of Americans" (Harrell, p. 15).

In 1924, Bosworth wrote a book on healing entitled *Christ the Healer*. In the 1973 reprint by Fleming H. Revell, Bosworth's son, said in the forward, "This book has become the greatest classic on the subject of divine healing and a textbook in the church Bible classes, Bible schools, and seminaries." Boggs agrees, saying Bosworth helped shape the theology of the healing movement and the practices of contemporary faith healers (Boggs, p. 13). According to historian Harrell, Bosworth was an important advisor to post-World War II healers, and his knowledge of techniques and healing theology was widely sought (Harrell, p. 15).

Amy Semple Macpherson

Amy Semple MacPherson (1890-1942) was the first female Pentecostal healing evangelist to receive world renown. Her escapades filled the front pages of major newspapers for several decades.

Amy was converted to Pentecostalism in 1907 at seventeen by an itinerant preacher, Robert Semple, who Zion had influenced. They were later married. Semple died in China, where they had gone to be missionaries. After her return to the United States, she married Harold MacPherson, a grocery salesman, but that marriage ended in divorce five years later.

The healing ministry of MacPherson began in tents and culminated in a temple. She started by conducting tent meetings from coast to coast, mainly preaching to the poor and "backward." In 1921, in San Diego, she began to attract large attendance and a great deal of attention. At one point, the authorities turned over the use of Balboa Park to her. She is reported to have prayed for the sick there for two days, from morning until night, until she fainted from exhaustion. Eventually, she settled in Los Angeles, where she built the huge Angelus Temple. Scandals dogged her path until her death but did not damage her popularity.

Sister MacPherson founded the L. I. F. E. (Lighthouse of International Foursquare Evangelism) Bible College, and the denomination officially titled "The International Church of the Foursquare Gospel." She was president until her death, when her son, Rolf MacPherson, took office.

Oral Roberts

Granville Oral Roberts, a king of faith healers, was born in Oklahoma in 1918. The youngest of five children, one of whom was incurably epileptic, Oral grew up a frail, shy introvert who frequently suffered from illness and from a stutter in his speech. As a teenager, he apparently contracted tuberculosis. His father, an itinerant farmer turned preacher, sent him to evangelist George Moncy, who was praying for the sick. Moncy prayed for Oral and commanded the disease to leave the boy's body. Roberts claims that both his stuttering and tuberculosis were instantly healed. He also claims that God spoke to him in an audible voice at that time in his life, saying, "Son, I am going to heal you and you are going to take My healing power to your generation." Two months later, at age 17 (1935), he began to preach. He was ordained in the

Pentecostal Holiness Church.

After pastoring several churches, traveling and taking courses from Oklahoma Baptist University and Philips University, God allegedly spoke to him again, telling him to be different from other men and go out and heal people. The year was 1947. He resigned from his pastorate, moved to Tulsa, and commenced to travel full-time, conducting revival campaigns. According to him, the power of God began to flow like a current of electricity through his "healing" right arm. He also described this sensation as liquid fire surging through his arm.

Once, during a tent service in Tulsa, a gunman, who later told police, "I don't know why I did it," pulled a gun and fired a shot at Roberts. It missed by two feet. The assailant was apprehended, arrested, and eventually released, but the incident gained national attention. Roberts' revivals prospered greatly because of the publicity. It was not the healing meetings but the shooting episode that made Oral Roberts well-known.

By the 1950s, Oral Roberts was the most successful of the faith healers. His first television program appeared in 1954. Later, he founded Oral Roberts University (1962), joined the Methodist Church (1968), and built a hospital called "The City of Hope." His son, Richard Roberts, became the heir to his father's ministry.

Benny Hinn

Benny Hinn was born in Israel in 1953 to a Greek father and an Armenian mother. He was reared in the Greek Orthodox Church.

He claims that God first appeared to him in Israel when he was 11 years old. At the age of 14, his family moved to Canada. In high school, he says he had visions of him preaching to huge crowds. He also claims that God healed him of a stuttering problem. Yet, he says he was converted in 1972 at a Kathryn Kuhlman service.

In 1983, he founded the Orlando Christian Center in Orlando, Florida. The name was later changed. In 1999, he resigned as pastor to continue his worldwide crusades and his daily television program, *This Is Your Day*.

Others

Many more faith healers, all of whom gained a following and attention, could be discussed. These include William Morrison Branham, Jack Cole, Rex Humbard, T. L. Osborne, O. L. Jaggers, Gordon Lindsay (born in Zion, Illinois, of parents who were disciples of John Alexander Dowie), W. J. Grant, A. A. Allen, Kathryn Kuhlman, Jimmy Swaggert, Kenneth Copeland, and Kenneth Hagin.

It should also be noted that on April 3, 1960, in St. Mark's Episcopal Church in Van Nuys, California, the rector, Dennis Bennett, claimed to have received the baptism of the Holy Spirit with the evidence of speaking in tongues. That marks the day the Pentecostal movement jumped denominational lines, emphasizing healing with it. The new movement within the traditional mainline denominations became known as the charismatic movement. While the charismatic movement is less sensational and less emotional, the theology of healing is virtually the same as its Pentecostal mother. The same could be said for the Roman Catholic charismatic movement, which began in a prayer meeting on the Notre Dame campus on April 8, 1967.

More recently, the "third wave" hit the United States. John Wimber, founder of the Vineyard in Fullerton, California, and author of *Power Evangelism,* has ridden on the wave's crest. Under the auspices of Peter Wagner, Wimber launched a course at Fuller Theological Seminary officially named MC510 and popularly called "Signs and Wonders." The course included an optional lab on divine healing. Ultimately, the reaction from the Fuller faculty caused the cancellation of MC510. *Christian Life* magazine did a nine-part report on "Signs and Wonders" (October 1982). Later, Wagner, professor of church growth at Fuller Seminary in Pasadena, California, authored a monthly column in *Christian Life* on the third wave.

According to those promoting this "supernatural phenomenon," the first wave was the Pentecostal movement at the turn of the century. The second wave was the charismatic movement in the mid-century, and the third wave was the outpouring of God's Spirit on thousands of traditional, evangelical, denominational churches in the form of supernatural healings. One conference on the third wave headlined their brochure with "Church Growth and the Third Wave: Supernatural Healing in the Local Church and Managing the Consequences of Signs and Wonders in the Church."

In the August 8, 1986, edition of *Christianity Today*, the cover story was on Wimber's Vineyard. The article concluded by asking, "Will the signs and wonders movement turn out to be ultimately just the latest trend from L.A.? Will it excite people for a few years, force incremental changes and then fade into obscurity, or will it turn out to be, as some expect, the source of a revolutionary revival? At this point, nobody can be sure" (*Christianity Today*, p. 22).

Summary: The theology of the healing movement began in the latter part of the 19th century in the writings of the A. J. Gordon and A. B. Simpson, but Charles Dowie was the true trailblazer for the theology and practice of healing theology. Dowie influenced Parham, who founded the Pentecostal movement, and Bosworth, who wrote *Christ The Healer*, which became the textbook for healing theology.

The modern healing movement continues to move, but what is its theology? More importantly, is its theology biblical?

Chapter 2

IS ALL SICKNESS FROM SATAN?

The healing movement blames Satan for sickness, not just some sickness, all sickness. According to them, God does not inflict disease on anyone. No less than Oral Roberts, the most famous faith healer of them all, has said, "When people teach that God afflicts human life with disease, they teach in direct contradiction to what Jesus and His disciples taught concerning the origin and work of affliction. The apostle Peter refers to sickness and disease as the 'oppression of the devil'" (Roberts, *If You Need Healing, Do These Things*, p. 16). He has also written, "In other words, sickness is from the devil (Acts 10:38). Healing is from God (Matt. 8:17)" (Roberts, *Master Key to Healing*, p. 10). Kenneth Hagin has written, "It is God's will to heal you because sickness comes from Satan, not from God, and God doesn't want His children to have anything that belongs to Satan" (Hagin, p. 13).

More than one faith healer has quoted the story of the woman with the bent back to prove that sickness is from Satan. Jesus healed the lady who had been bent over for eighteen years and could not straighten up (Lk. 13:10-13). When challenged for healing on the Sabbath, Jesus explained that Satan had bound her for eighteen years (Lk. 13:16).

Does all disease come from the devil and only the devil? Many, if not all, in the divine healing movement from the latter part of the nineteenth century to the present have claimed that such is the case. Are they right? To answer this pertinent question, consider what the Scripture says concerning the source of sickness.

Satan can Afflict a Person with Sickness

The Old Testament In the Old Testament, there is only one example of sickness inflicted by Satan. Job 1:1 says that Job was blameless and upright. Nevertheless, Satan accused Job before God of only obeying Him because of what he was personally getting out of it, namely material prosperity (Job 1:6-10). He further charged that if God took away the benefits, Job would curse Him to His face (Job 1:11).

To prove His point, God permitted Satan to do anything he wished with Job's possessions, but he could not lay a hand on Job's person (Job 1:12). Job promptly lost his property and his children, but he did not curse God (Job 1:22). Then Satan charged that if Job lost his health, as well as his wealth, he would lose his faithfulness to God. So, God allowed Satan to take Job's health. The Scripture says, "Then Satan struck Job with painful boils from the sole of his foot to the crown of his head" (Job 1:7).

The story of Job conclusively demonstrates that Satan can afflict a person with sickness. Apparently, in the case of a child of God, he has to have the Father's permission, but he has the ability. The question is not, however, "can he inflict a person with sickness?" but "Is he the source of all sickness?"

The New Testament: While there is only one passage in the Old Testament that attributes sickness to Satan, several passages in the New Testament seem to say that disease comes from the devil. For example, in Luke 13, Jesus healed a woman who had a "spirit of infirmity" for eighteen years. She was bent over and could not raise herself up (Lk. 13:11). The ruler of the synagogue complained that Christ healed her on the Sabbath. In His answer to His opponents, Christ said, "Satan had bound this woman for eighteen years."

Christ also said, "Hypocrites! Does not each of you on the Sabbath loose his ox or his donkey from the stall and lead it away to water it? So ought not this woman, being a daughter of Abraham whom Satan has bound—think of it—for eighteen years, be loosed from this bond on the Sabbath?" (Lk. 13:15-16). The Lord contrasted their piety for a bound, thirsty donkey to His compassion for the sick woman. There is an obvious contrast between 1) the ox or donkey and the daughter of Abraham, 2) the stall and Satan, and 3) one day and eighteen years. The punch in the comparison is between the one day and the eighteen years. There is no doubt that Christ is saying, at least in this case, that this woman's infirmity was from the devil. The implication is that all such problems are.

Peter said something similar. In his sermon at Cornelius' house, he said, "God anointed Jesus of Nazareth with the Holy Spirit and with power who went about doing good and healing all who were oppressed by the devil, for God was with Him" (Acts 10:38). It is possible that the phrase "healing all who the devil oppressed" is a reference to casting out demons, but the Greek word translated "healing" is used repeatedly in the New Testament of the healing of disease and never of exorcism. Peter's statement, then, must refer to the healing of disease. This expression does not prove that all disease is from the devil, but it does say that there are diseases that come from Satan.

Paul said his "thorn in the flesh" was a messenger of Satan (2 Cor. 12:7). There has been great speculation since ancient times as to the nature of Paul's thorn. "Flesh" may be taken literally for the body or figuratively for the sinful nature. In this passage, it should be taken literally. If so, Paul's thorn in the flesh was some physical infirmity. He called it a "messenger of Satan," meaning he sent it. As in the case of Peter's statement in Acts 10, this does not prove that all sickness is from Satan, but it does attribute this one to him, which indicates that Satan can afflict people with infirmities.

Sickness can Come from God

Those who claim that sickness comes from Satan, and only Satan, conveniently overlook the passages that teach that sickness can come from God. For example, Deuteronomy 32:39 states, "Now seeing that I, even I am He and there is no God beside Me; I kill and I make alive; I wound, and I heal; nor is there anyone who can deliver from My hand." The point is that life, health, and victory in war are in God's hand and so are death, disease, and defeat. Everything that happened to a child of Israel happened by the power of God. God gives woes and well-being. Other passages teach this same concept.

"Who is he who speaks and it comes to pass, when the Lord has not commanded it? Is it not from the mouth of the Most High that woe and well-being proceed?" (Lam. 3:37, 38).

"Behold, happy is the man whom God corrects; therefore do not despise the chastening of the Almighty. For He bruises, but He binds up; He wounds, but His hands make whole" (Job 5:17-18).

To be specific, blindness and death can come from God. When Moses objected to going to Pharaoh because he was not eloquent but slow of speech (Ex. 4:10), God said to Him, "Who has made man's mouth? Or who makes the mute, the deaf, the seeing, or the blind? Have not I, the Lord?" (Ex. 4:11).

To illustrate His power, God once made Moses sick! God commanded Moses to tell Pharaoh to let His people go. Moses' first excuse was that the people would not believe that God had appeared to him (Ex. 4:1). After miraculously transforming a rod into a serpent, God told Moses to put his hand in his bosom (Ex. 4:6). When he did and pulled it out again, it was leprous. God immediately healed it (Ex. 4:7), but this incident indicates that sickness can come directly from God.

To Judge Why would God deliberately make someone sick? One answer is judgment. God sometimes afflicts His children with sickness because of their sins. Paul told the Corinthians that because they were partaking of the Lord's Table in an unworthy manner, some were weak, some were sick, and some were dead (1 Cor. 11:30).

The Old Testament reveals several cases of God directly striking someone with leprosy because of their sin. Miriam was stricken with leprosy for questioning Moses' leadership (Num. 12:1-15). Uzziah encountered the same fate because of his pride (2 Chron. 26:16-21). Although the text does not say Gehazi's sudden case of leprosy was from the Lord, it was (2 Kings 5:20-27). In Jahoram's case, God used an incurable intestinal disease, which he suffered from for two years before he died (2 Chron. 21:18, 19). God also used insanity (Dan. 4:28-31) and an unspecified illness (2 Sam. 12:1-23).

In the New Testament, blindness came straight from the hand of the Lord on an unsaved sorcerer named Elymas as a judgment on his interference with the ministry of the Word (Acts 13:4-12). In both the Old and New Testaments, God used death as an instrument of judgment (Ex. 12:29-30; Lev. 10:1; 2; 2 Kings 19:35; Acts 5:1-11; 12:23).

To Teach Judgment is not the only reason sickness can come from God. He sometimes uses illness and injury to teach. When Jacob wrestled with God, God put his hip out of joint. Jacob walked with a limp for the remainder of his life as a reminder of his encounter with God (Gen. 32:22-32). God refused to remove Paul's thorn to teach him humility and dependence (2 Cor. 12:1-10).

To Glorify God God also uses sickness to glorify Himself. The blind beggar of John 9 was born blind, not because he or his parents sinned, but so that God's works could be revealed when Jesus healed him in his adult life (Jn. 9:1-3).

People today sometimes have a hard time accepting the idea that sickness can be beneficial because they have been conditioned to make the avoidance of pain and the experience of pleasure the goal of life. People today are hedonists—for them, pleasure is the highest good. Christians have absorbed this philosophy to the point that today it is intolerable to suppose that pain may be within the purposes of God. America is obsessed with health to the point that it borders on sickness!

According to biblical Christianity, sin—not pain—is the greatest evil, and spiritual maturity—not pleasure—is the greatest goal. The ultimate is the glory of God. Thus, God arranges everything to develop growth, character, Christlikeness, and godliness.

Summary: While sickness can come from Satan, it can also come from and can be used by God to accomplish His purposes.

The reality is that affliction can come directly from God, or He may choose to use Satan as the means. Ultimately, sickness is allowed by the sovereign God of the universe. Interesting. Satan is often God's servant (Job; Paul's thorn in the flesh; and even 1 Sam. 16:14). Calvin captured this truth when he wrote, "This is the comfort of the believer, to understand that the heavenly Father does so embrace all things with His power that nothing befalls but by His appointment; and that he received into God's keeping and cannot be touched with any harm of water or fire or sword, that so far as it please God the governor to give them place ... and from hence proceeds the boldness of the saints. For when they call to mind that the devil and all the rout of the wicked are so everywhere hold in by the hand of God as with a bridle that they can neither conceive any mischief against us, nor put it into train when they have conceived it, nor can stir one finger to bring it to pass, but so far as He shall suffer, yea so far as He shall command, and that they are not only held fast with fetters but also compelled with bridle to do service, here they have abundant springs of constellation" (Calvin, *The Institutes.* I, chap. 17, para. 11).

Whenever affliction or sickness comes from God, or at least is allowed by God, it is for a positive purpose. Boggs suggests that in the Scripture, suffering of all kinds has meaning, including the ten plagues (Ex. 7-11), the leprosy of Miriam (Num. 12:10), the enteritis of King Jehoram (2 Chron. 21:18), the leprosy of Gehazi (2 Kings 5:27), the death of David's child (2 Sam. 12:18) and of Eli's sons (1 Sam. 2:34), the undeserved misfortunes of Joseph (Gen. 45:5-7), the crucifixion of Jesus Christ (Mk. 14:35-36; Rom. 5:6-12), the imprisonment of Paul (Phil. 1:12, 19) and his thorn in the flesh (2 Cor. 12:7).

Boggs says, "The human family may be helped in its growth toward Christian maturity, both by affliction and the struggle against affliction. There is no real contradiction between the two. The same God who sent the winds, rains, and floods to beat upon the house of life also sends His Son to teach men how to build their houses on a foundation that will withstand these onslaughts. As P. T. Forsythe says, 'God ordained disease for the purpose of being resistant; He ordained the resistance that from the conflict men might come out stronger and more full of resources and dominion over nature'" (Boggs, p. 144).

In his autobiography, Richard Baxter, the famous seventeenth-century English preacher, wrote: "I have lain in above forty years constant weakness and almost constant pain," but he came to regard his pain as an invaluable mercy. He continued, "I humbly bless His gracious Providence, who ... trained me up in the school of affliction and taught me the cross of Christ so soon." He adds that his illness made him "live and preach in some continual expectation of death, supposing that I had not long to live [which] made me study and preach things necessary and a little stirred up my sluggish heart to speak to sinners with some compassion, as a dying man to dying men." He concludes, "The great benefit that I have found in former afflictions assures me that they come from Fatherly love; yea, have been so merciful a work of Providence, as I can be sufficiently thankful for: what have they done to keep me away, and call me to repentance, and to improve my short and precious time, and bid me work while it is day? What have they done to keep me from covetousness, pride and idleness, and tell me where I must place all my hope, and how little the world and all of its vanities do signify? And shall I think the same God who intended me good by all the rest of the afflictions of my life doth now intend my hurt at last? Experience condemns my impatience" (Baxter, pp. 399-400).

As someone has said, "The Lord sometimes allows His saints to be sharpened on the devil's grindstone."

God uses suffering, including sickness, to perfect, and He also uses affliction to prepare for service. J. I. Packer has observed,

"Paul perceived, however, that the thorn was given him not for punishment, but for protection. Physical weakness guarded him against spiritual weakness. The worst diseases are those of the spirit. Pride, conceit, arrogance, bitterness, and self-confidence are far worse, and they damage us far more than any malfunctioning of our bodies. The thorn was a prophylactic against pride. Says Paul, 'To keep me from being too elated by the abundance of revelations.' Seeing that was so, he could accept it as a wise provision on the part of his Lord.... God uses chronic pain and weakness, along with other sorts of affliction, as His chisel for sculpturing our souls. Felt weaknesses deepen dependence on Christ for strength each day. The weaker we feel, the harder we lean. The harder we lean, the stronger we grow spiritually, even while our bodies waste away. To live with your complaint uncomplainingly, being kept sweet, patient and free of heart to love and help others, even though every day you feel less than good is true sanctification. It is true healing for the spirit; it is the supreme victory of grace in your life (Packer, pp. 15-16).

The simple reality is that there can be sickness where there is no sin. God can allow the sickness to prepare His servant for service. Hudson Taylor's longstanding heart ailment was not associated with sin. It caused him much anguish, and yet he could agree with the man who said, "Health is the best thing in the world except sickness." Seeing that both the inception and the development of the China Inland Mission were associated with physical breakdowns, his times of physical weakness were not times of spiritual decline. On the contrary, they were commonly the times of his closest communion with the Lord.

Let me illustrate. Boggs tells the story of a man named Frank A. Brown, who, for many years, was a veteran missionary of the Presbyterian Church in China. When it came time for his retirement, he was stricken with leprosy. Those who knew him best would instantly repudiate that this was just punishment for his sin. As Boggs puts it, "Even less than Job did he deserve such a misfortune." Brown spent no time in self-pity in the leprosarium at Carville, Louisiana. Instead, he wrote a book about his wife's missionary activities. The book was designed to inspire young women to seek such a career. He pointed out that people in the leprosarium were lonely and desperately needed spiritual ministry. Brown believed that his time in the leprosarium was perhaps his life's most glorious missionary opportunity.

Chapter 3

IS IT ALWAYS GOD'S WILL TO HEAL?

In his book, *Where Is God When It Hurts*, Philip Yancey tells of an incident in the life of Claudia Claxton. Soon after she was married, Claudia contracted Hodgkin's Disease and was given a fifty percent chance to live. When she was in the hospital, many of her friends stopped by to encourage her. Here is Yancey's account of one visit: "Another lady who had faithfully watched Oral Roberts, Kathryn Kuhlman, and 'The 700 Club' over the years had dropped by. She told Claudia that healing was the only escape. 'Sickness is never God's will,' she insisted. 'The Bible says as much. The devil is at work and God will wait until you can muster up enough faith to believe Him that you will be healed. Remember, Claudia, faith can move mountains, including Hodgkin's Disease. Truly believe that you will be healed and God will answer your prayer'" (Yancey, p. 13).

The lady visiting Claudia Claxton claimed it was God's will for all to be healed. According to her, sickness is of Satan; disease is of the devil; healing and health are of God.

Traditionally, faith healers have claimed that good health for all people is always God's will. In his book *Christ the Healer*, Bosworth has a chapter entitled "Is Healing for All?" In it, he says, "The greatest barrier to the faith of many seeking bodily healing in our day is the uncertainty in their minds as to it being the will of God to heal *all*. Nearly everyone knows that God does heal *some*, but much in modern theology keeps the people from knowing what the Bible clearly teaches—that healing is provided for all" (Bosworth, p. 41, italics his). "Let the sick go through the Gospels and note the *alls* and the *everys*, and they will see that the redemptive blessing of healing was for *all* and that no one ever appealed in vain to Jesus for healing. There never was a multitude large enough to have in it, even one that Jesus wanted to remain sick, and would not heal" (Bosworth, p. 49, italics his). "If sickness, as some think, is the will of God for His faithful children, then it is a sin for them even to desire to be well, to say nothing of spending thousands of dollars to defeat His purpose. I truly thank God for all the help that has ever come to sufferers through the physician, the surgeon, the hospital, and the trained nurse, but if sickness is the will of God, then, to quote one writer, 'Every physician is a lawbreaker; every trained nurse is defying the Almighty; every hospital is a house of rebellion instead of a house of mercy' and instead of *supporting* hospitals, we are to do our utmost to *close* every one" (Bosworth, p. 59, italics his).

Oral Roberts follows the tradition. He has said, "I believe and know beyond the shadow of a doubt that it is God's highest and perfect will to heal you from every affliction in your body.... Some talk about sickness being a blessing, but I will take healing for my blessing every time" (Roberts, *If You Need Healing, Do These Things*, pp. 22, 23).

Kenneth Hagin also echoes this teaching. He has stated, "I am fully convinced—I would die saying it is so—that it is the plan of our Father God, in His great love and in His great mercy, that no believer should ever be sick and that every believer should live his full life span down here on earth; and that every believer should finally just fall asleep in Jesus.... I'm going to state it again. It is NOT God our heavenly Father's will that Christians should suffer with cancer and with other dread diseases that bring pain and anguish. It IS God's will that we live our full length of time on earth" (Hagin, p. 21, 24).

Kenneth Copeland also teaches that it is the will of God for all to be healed. He has stated, "Many people think God wants them to stay sick so He can get glory out of their travails; but that kind of thinking is a lie straight from the pit of hell.... You can know beyond doubt that God's will is for every person in Jesus Christ to be healed and made well . . . God wants every believer to be healed and whole" (Copeland, *You Are Healed*, pp. 9, 19).

Ernest Angley agrees, saying, "God's will is for everyone to receive healing. Don't ever let the devil make you doubt this!" (Angley, p. 22).

Many healers have pointed out that Jesus healed "all" the sick (Lk. 4:40; 6:19). Christ even gave the twelve apostles the power to heal "all kinds of sickness and all kinds of disease" (Mt. 10:1) when He sent them to the lost sheep of the house of Israel. Luke records that at least on one occasion, "all" were healed (Acts 5:16).

What is the will of God concerning sickness? Is it His will to always heal? Many verses are used to support the claim that it is always God's will to heal. Consider the ones most often used and a few pertinent to the discussion that are never used, at least by those in the healing movement.

God never Promised to Always Heal

Exodus 15:26 Bosworth points to Exodus 15, saying that in this passage, "God gave His first promise to heal. The promise was for all" (Bosworth, p. 43). Does Exodus 15 teach that God promised to heal all?

Moses led the children of Israel out of Egypt across the Red Sea and into the wilderness of Shur. Then they ran out of water. For three days, they had no water to drink (Ex. 15:22). Finally, when they did find water at Marah, they could not drink it because it was bitter. The people began to murmur (Ex. 15:22-24).

Moses cried to the Lord, who showed him a tree which, when cast into the waters, "the waters were made sweet" (Ex. 15:25). The Lord then said, "If you diligently heed the voice of the Lord your God to do what is right in His sight, give ear to His commandments and keep all His statutes, I will put none of these diseases on you which I have brought on the Egyptians for I am the Lord who heals you" (Ex. 15:26).

The diseases referred to were the plagues in general, but especially the turning of water into blood, which made it undrinkable. Beyond the immediate situation, the Lord claims to be the one who heals. The diseases and the healing are not limited to physical illness, but there is no doubt that sickness is included. Murray captures the message well: "He had preserved them from the diseases of Egypt, the death of the firstborn and the destruction which overtook the Egyptians, so would He be their deliverer in every trouble which should befall them" (Murray, p. 168). Similar promises can be found elsewhere in the Pentateuch (Ex. 23:25; Deut. 7:15).

The question is, "Is Exodus 15:26 a promise that God will always heal?" More specifically, "Does it apply to Christians today?" The answer is "No." Exodus 15:26 and similar verses in the Pentateuch are conditional promises to Israel. Today, God is dealing with the church to whom He has promised all spiritual blessings (Eph. 1:3). Richard Mayhue's comment on Exodus 15:26 puts these promises in their proper biblical perspective: "We do not currently expect any of the judgments promised to Israel (Deut. 28:15-68), and because we are not enjoying any of these blessings that were enjoyed during her forty-year wilderness journey (such as daily rations of manna and quail in Exod. 16:1-21, or clothes and shoes that never wore out as in Deut. 29:5), the conditional promise to Israel in Exodus 15:26 does not apply to the church today. God has been, is and always will be capable of healing any disease at any time, but only according to His revealed will in Scripture. Exodus 15:26 is simply not a promise for believers today (Mayhue, p. 58).

Psalm 103:3 Psalm 103 opens with David praising God for all His blessings and benefits. These include forgiveness (103:3), healing (103:3), and deliverance from destruction (103:4), etc. The Hebrew word translated "disease" is used five times in the Old Testament and always refers to physical disease. David is praising God for healing.

From what disease did David suffer? The Bible does not record David ever having an incurable sickness. It reveals that David's sin was responsible for physical ailments (Ps. 32:1-5; 38:3). David's guilt produced physical effects (Ps. 32:3-4; 38:3-8). His confession and repentance brought relief (Ps. 51:8; 32:7, 10).

The issue is not whether or not God healed David. It is, "Is Psalm 103:3 teaching God heals all disease all the time? The answer is again 'No." David was merely rehearsing the fact that God had healed all his prior sicknesses. That does not mean He will do the same for everyone.

Peter said, "Lord, if it is You, command me to come to You on the water" (Mt 14:28). Jesus told him to "Come" and Peter "walked on the water to go to Jesus" (Mt. 14:29), but it is not the will of God for all to walk on water.

John 14:12 In the Upper Room before His crucifixion, Jesus told the apostles, "Most assuredly I say to you, he who believes in Me, the works that I do, he will do also and greater works than those he will do because I go to My Father" (Jn. 14:12). Faith healers often quote this verse to justify their activities. What does John 14:12 mean? To whom was Jesus speaking? What exactly did He promise them? Does this verse mean God always heals?

To whom was the Lord speaking, those present or all believers? The verse says, "he who believes in Me." An examination of the context indicates that He was speaking to the eleven disciples (Jn. 14:9 ff.). Judas had already departed (Jn. 13:30). The Lord uses the pronoun "you" throughout the passage to refer to the apostles.

In John 14:12, He says, "I say to *you.*" It would be unnatural and highly unlikely for Him to switch from addressing the disciples to all believers. John 14:12, then, is addressed to the apostles who are identified as those who believe in Christ.

What did Christ mean when He said that the apostles would do greater works than He did? He could not mean greater in quantity (Jn. 21:25) nor greater in quality. The apostles did not perform miracles of creation. Christ created food, fish, and wine; the apostles did not. Christ also performed miracles in nature, like calming the sea, whereas the apostles did not.

The next phrase is the key to understanding Christ's statement: "Because I go to My Father." What were the disciples able to do that Christ did, and they would even do greater than He did because He went to the Father? The answer has to do with the ministry of the Holy Spirit. Jesus taught that the Holy Spirit would not come until He left (Jn. 7:39, 16:7). After Christ ascended, He sent the Holy Spirit. Thus, when the apostles preached the gospel and people believed, they received the Holy Spirit, a greater work than physical healing and a greater work than Christ did when He walked on the earth.

Commentator Godet put it like this: "What Peter did on Pentecost, St. Paul throughout the whole world, a simple preacher, a plain believer bringing down the Spirit into some heart, Jesus could not do during His earthly sojourn" (Godet, Vol. II, p. 139).

Leon Morris, also a commentator, says something similar. "What Jesus means we may see in the narratives of the Acts. There, there are a few miracles of healing, but the emphasis is on the mighty works of conversion. On the day of Pentecost alone, more believers were added to the little band of believers than throughout Christ's entire earthly ministry. There, we see a literal fulfillment of "greater works than these shall you do." During His lifetime, the Son of God was confined in His influence to a comparatively small sector of Palestine. After His departure, His followers were able to work in widely scattered places and influence much larger numbers of men. But they did it all on the basis of Christ's return to the Father" (Morris, p. 646).

John 5:20-21 confirms this interpretation. Like John 14:12, John 5:20 refers to "works" and "greater works." Verse 21 explains that the "works" include raising the dead and the "greater works" give spiritual life.

Jesus sent out the seventy with the power to perform miracles. When they returned rejoicing in the physical miracles, Christ exhorted them, saying, "Do not rejoice in this that the spirits are subject to you, but rather rejoice because your names were written in heaven" (Lk. 10:20).

John 14:12 does not promise that Christians today will do the same or greater physical miracles than Christ. It certainly does not teach that God will always heal.

Hebrews 13:8 Hebrews 13:8 is probably the most often quoted verse in the Bible by faith healers today. That verse says, "Jesus Christ is the same yesterday, today, and forever." They reason that since God healed in the past and never changed, He must also heal in the same way today. Is that what Hebrews 13:8 is teaching?

The answer is "No." Hebrews 13:8 simply says that Christ's *person* never changes; *He* is the same today as He was yesterday and will be the same way forever. That does not mean His *program* never changes or His will is the same for everyone.

God's program has changed. In the Old Testament, the Jews brought lambs to the Tabernacle on Saturday. Today, believers gather on Sunday to hear the preaching of the Word and to observe the Lord's Supper. In the Old Testament, God supernaturally supplied the children of Israel with food and clothes during their forty-year trip through the wilderness, but He did not do that throughout Old Testament history, nor did He do it during the New Testament period, and He does not do that today.

God's will for individuals is not the same. In John 21, the Lord told Peter he would die violently (Jn. 21:18, 19). When Peter asked about John, Jesus told him, "If I will that he remain until I come, what is that to you?" (Jn. 21:22). In Acts 12, both Peter and James trusted God for protection. Peter was miraculously released from prison; James was executed. God's person never changes, but He has different wills for different individuals.

Furthermore, this verse is not talking about healing. It does not even include Christ's healing activity. That is obvious, for the verse says, "forever." The Lord will not heal forever (Rev. 22:1-5). Just as it is not true to say that God healed in the past and, therefore, He will heal forever, so it is not true to say that He healed in the past and He heals today.

In conclusion, God did heal through His power, but He never promised to heal every individual in every age. The thesis that all sickness is from Satan and it is God's will to heal all is simply not true. Granted, there are occasions when Christ and the apostles healed all the sick *who were present*, but there were also occasions when not all were healed! For example, although many sick people were in the five porches of the pool of Bethesda, Jesus only healed one (Jn. 5:1-9). There were occasions when Paul could not, or at least did not, heal (2 Tim. 4:20). The evidence is clear that neither Jesus nor His disciples healed all the sick all the time. God has never promised always to heal. There is no guarantee in the Bible that He will heal all, all the time.

People in the Will of God have been Sick

The Old Testament There were saints in the Bible who were in the will of God but who were also physically ill and God did not choose to heal them. In his old age, Isaac went blind (Gen. 27:1). He was never healed. After Jacob wrestled with God, he walked the rest of his life with a limp (Gen. 32:25 ff.). He also later got sick and died without being cured (Gen. 49:1 ff.). There were other such cases in the Old Testament (1 Kings 14:4), including Elisha, who healed others but got sick and was not cured; rather, he died (2 Kings 13:14).

The New Testament The same thing happened in the New Testament. Paul left Trophimus at Miletus sick (2 Tim. 4:20). Paul himself is the classic example of a sick saint in the will of God without healing. He said that lest he should be exalted above measure because of the abundance of revelation he had been permitted to have, there was given to him a thorn in the flesh (2 Cor. 12:7). There is a debate over the exact nature of the thorn, but most have concluded that it was a physical infirmity, probably a problem with his eyes. At any rate, he prayed for it to be removed three times, and each time, God said, "No." Instead, God told Paul His grace was sufficient for him (2 Cor. 12:8-9).

Summary: A study of the Scripture on the subject of the will of God concerning healing reveals that God promised to heal and did, but He never promised always to heal and some in His will got sick without being healed. Therefore, to tell people that it is always God's will to heal is wrong and dangerous.

Larry and Alice Parker were the parents of six children. Wesley, their oldest son, had diabetes, for which he received regular insulin injections. On a hot summer night in August of 1973, the Parkers walked the aisle of a Barstow, California church with Wesley, who was then eleven years of age. Daniel Badilla, an itinerant Mexican-American preacher, anointed Wesley with oil, laid hands on him, prayed, and pronounced him cured. Larry gleefully entered Wesley's insulin log: "Praise God, our son is healed."

Wesley was not healed. The next morning, he decided to test his blood sugar. Finding it positive, he started to take his usual insulin shot when his father grabbed the instruments, squeezed out the insulin and broke off the hypodermic needle. The Parkers "claimed" Wesley's healing and blamed the blood sugar level on Satan. Without insulin injections, however, it was not long before

Wesley began to suffer nausea and severe stomach cramps.

As Wesley's condition began to deteriorate, the Parkers, their pastor, and many of their friends gathered to pray for his recovery. The symptoms persisted. By the second day, Wesley was lapsing into periods of unconsciousness.

Growing increasingly concerned for her son's health, Alice Parker decided that Wesley should be taking his insulin after all. Her husband prevented her from giving the boy any more insulin. He explained that he had cast the demons, who were the cause of the problem, out of Wesley's body. He was sure that the youngster would now begin to regain his health. "I knew then the diabetes was caused by two demons and that we could no longer give insulin without inviting the demons back," he said.

They prayed without ceasing for Wesley's recovery from Tuesday morning until Wednesday afternoon. The lad did not get better. The pastor recommended that they call a doctor. Someone finally notified the police, but it was too late. When the police arrived on Wednesday afternoon, Wesley was dead. He had suffered a painful, lingering death.

The parents, however, were unperturbed. "He is going to be resurrected," they announced. They refused to permit an autopsy, and though they later consented, they at first refused to have the body embalmed. Alice declared, "Christ is going to have to replace the blood that's full of sugar anyway, so it might as well be embalming fluid. If we hadn't done it, people might say he was in a deep coma and not believe the miracle."

A resurrection service was planned and announced. Numerous curiosity-seekers and friends showed up for the ceremony to be held in the funeral chapel. They laid hands on the body, and prayed with enthusiasm, but Wesley remained lifeless.

Undaunted, the father concluded that his son, like Lazarus in John 11, would rise from the dead on the fourth day. Nothing happened. Nevertheless, they extended their vigil. They still had faith that Wesley would return healthy and happy.

Their pastor was horrified. Many of the Christians concluded that the Parkers had erred. The events surrounding Wesley's death began to attract reporters. Amid the uproar, the local authorities charged the Parkers with manslaughter and child abuse. In July of 1974, a jury found the Parkers guilty of involuntary manslaughter. They were sentenced to five years on probation. One of the conditions of their probation was that they report to their probation officer any illnesses or injuries affecting their other children.

That case received nationwide coverage by the news media because of its sensational nature. Countless other cases have not received publicity but are just as tragic. In April of 1978, Dustin Graham Gilmore, age fifteen months, had flu-like symptoms. His father, David, took him to his church and the pastor prayed that the infant would be healed. According to the doctrine of their church, if David had sought medical treatment for his son, he would have been demonstrating a lack of faith. So, David and his wife followed the church's counsel and simply and solely prayed for their son.

They prayed faithfully over the next several weeks as little Dustin's temperature climbed. When he no longer responded to sounds, they prayed even harder. Then, Dustin went blind. On May 15, 1978, the Gilmores found their son dead in his bed. Again, they prayed, this time for his resurrection, but Dustin remained dead. An autopsy revealed that he died from a form of meningitis that could easily have been treated.

After five years of silence, Gilmore decided to make his story public because he knew of twelve other children who had died under similar circumstances. In printing his story, the *Chicago Tribune* indicated that people from his church had spread to five states (Indiana, Illinois, Michigan, Ohio, and Kentucky). The number of deaths because of that church's teaching in those five states totaled fifty-two.

Because God has not promised to heal every person in every case, believers must realize that God's will for health and death is different for each individual and accept God's will for their individual life (Jn. 21:15-22). George Mueller once asked, "Lord, why am I afflicted like this?" He said the answer to his heart was, "My child, this is the best thing for you. If there were any better thing, I would give it to you because I love you." The simple reality is God's will is different for every individual.

In the June 1980 issue of *Our Daily Bread*, Dennis DeHaan told how a Christian providentially escaped death. An unexpected delay in New York kept him from catching Flight 191 in Chicago, which crashed with all 254 passengers aboard. As a result of that article, he received a letter from a reader who said, "I just let you know about one of God's great saints who ran to make Flight 191—and made it." Edward E. Elliott was the beloved Garden Grove Orthodox Presbyterian Church pastor in California. His plane from Pennsylvania was late, and a friend who had accompanied him to Chicago said he saw him dashing forward in the terminal to make a connection. It was the will of God for one saint to miss Flight 191; it was the will of God for another to catch it.

Chapter 4

DID CHRIST DIE FOR SICKNESS?

The heart of the healing theology is the doctrine of healing in the atonement. The healing movement teaches that Jesus Christ died for sickness *as* He died for sin, that is, as a substitute. Apparently, this doctrine was first suggested by A. J. Gordon and became the cornerstone of the ministry of the faith healers. Boggs writes, "So far as I have been able to discover, the theology that healing for all faithful Christians is in the atonement originated with a well-known Boston theologian and preacher, A. J. Gordon. Dr. Gordon set forth in his book, *The Ministry of Healing* (1882), what he regarded as the Scriptural foundation of divine healing. Matthew's quotation from Isaiah's suffering servant poem (Isa. 53:4), which reads, 'He took our infirmities and bore our diseases' (Matt. 8:17), figured prominently in his reasoning. He observed that the Scripture 'seemed to teach that Christ bore the sicknesses of mankind vicariously' and that 'therefore it was possible to secure healing in the same way as forgiveness of sins.' But whereas Dr. Gordon's language shows that he regarded this as a tentative suggestion, more in the sphere of inquiring and investigation than in the sphere of dogma, his successors developed his suggestion into what Bingham calls the 'Magna Carta' of the entire healing theory" (Boggs, p. 81).

Bosworth, who is said to have written the textbook on healing used in many Bible colleges, said in his book on healing: "After being sufficiently enlightened, our attitude toward *sickness* should be the same as our attitude toward sin. Our purpose to have our *body* healed should be as definite as our purpose to have our *soul* healed. We should not ignore any part of the gospel. Our Substitute bore both our sins and our sicknesses that we might be delivered from them. Christ's bearing of our sins and sicknesses is surely a valid reason for trusting Him *now* for deliverance from both. When in prayer, we definitely commit to God the forgiveness of our *sins*, we are to believe on the authority of His Word that our prayer is heard. We are to do the same with praying for healing" (Bosworth, p. 8, italics his). "Since disease is part of the curse, its true remedy must be the cross, for who can remove the curse but God, and how can God *justly* do it except by substitution" (Bosworth, p. 15, italics his). "The purpose of this sermon is to prove that healing is provided by the atonement and is, therefore, part of the gospel which Christ commanded to be preached to 'all the world' to 'aord Jesus Christ. He not only took our sins, He took our infirmities and bore our sicknesses" (Hagin, *In Jesus' Name*, p. t of all that which I also received: that Christ died for our sins according to the Scriptures, and that He was buried, and that He rose again thto as having been born by Him on the cross. Paul's testimony is that God the Father made God the Son to be sin for us, not sickness for us (II Cor. 5:21)" (Lightner, p. 41).

According to Lightner, this observation also includes the Old Testament. He states, "Not only do the prophecies concerning the death of Christ (and there are many more than are here stated) fail to deal with the matter of bodily healing, but the types of His death fail to do so as well. Not one of these types of His death, and there are at least sixteen, reveal anything about bodily healing either in its primary meaning or in the type it represents. There is nothing about bodily healing in the offerings or sacrifices of the Old Testament of which Christ became the perfect offering. They all deal with the remission of sins, not sickness. Why did these Old Testament saints not know anything about physical healing in the coming redemption" (Lightner, pp. 41-42).

The Bible, then, in many passages in both the Old and New Testaments, teaches that Christ died for sins without mentioning anything about Him dying for sickness. It is also interesting to note that the church was commanded to preach the forgiveness of sins based on Christ's death. After Christ died and rose, He explained His death and resurrection to the disciples (Lk. 24:46). Then He commissioned them to preach repentance and remission of sins (Lk. 24:47). He did not command them to heal the sick. That is striking in light of the fact that when the Lord sent out the twelve to the lost sheep of the house of Israel, he did tell them to heal the sick (Mt. 10:5-8)!

In his study of divine healing in the Bible, Lightner points all of this out and adds that when the Lord spoke of the coming of the Holy Spirit, He said nothing about healing the sick (Jn. 16:8). Then he adds, "Both of these passages (Matt. 28:19 and John 16:8) take us to a very strategic point in Christ's ministry. He was about to leave His disciples. If there was ever a time when they needed direction, it was at this time. They had been dependent upon Him, possibly too much, and now He was to go away and they were about to walk alone. Their last command from their captain did not include anything about physical healing. Christ did not command His disciples to heal as part of God's salvation/gospel. Rather, He commanded them to love one another, which was evidence of their love for God. He said, 'These things I command you that you love one another'" (Jn. 15:17; Lightner, pp. 42-43).

Christ did not Die for Sickness as He did for Sin

Isaiah 53 Proponents of healing in the atonement argue that Isaiah 53, one of the greatest passages in the Bible on the death of Christ, says that He bore our griefs and carried our sorrows (Isa. 53:4) and that by His stripes we were healed (Isa. 53:5). Is not that passage teaching that physical healing is in the atonement?

The answer is "No." The inspired interpretation of these verses in the New Testament indicates they are not teaching that Christ *died* for sickness. In Matthew 8, Christ healed the sick (Mt. 8:14-16). Matthew, under the inspiration of the Holy Spirit, says He did that "that it might be fulfilled which was spoken by Isaiah the prophet" (Mt. 8:17). Then he quotes Isaiah 53:4, "He Himself took our infirmities and bore our sicknesses" (Mt. 8:17). This passage does not say Christ died or suffered for our infirmities; it says He "took" them. The same Greek word translated "took" is used in Matthew 5:40 of taking a coat. Likewise, the Lord took away their sicknesses by healing them. That does not mean that He died for them as a substitute, as He died for sin.

Furthermore, the word "bore" is never used in the New Testament regarding Christ's atoning death. It is used in Galatians 6:2, where Christ says, "Bear one another's burdens." The idea is to help people, to relieve them. It has nothing to do with atonement. Likewise, the Lord "bore" people's sicknesses by relieving them. He did not bear sicknesses in Capernaum in a substitutionary way; instead, He removed sickness.

Besides, the obvious meaning of the passage in Matthew 8 is that Christ fulfilled Isaiah 53:4 *in His life*, not His death. There is no way Christ could have fulfilled Isaiah 53:4 in His death because He fulfilled it before He died!

What about Isaiah's statement that by His stripes, we were healed? Peter does not claim to quote Isaiah, but there is no doubt that the passage was in his mind when he wrote 1 Peter 2. In talking about Christ dying for sin, he says, "Who Himself bore our sins in His own body on the tree, that we, having died to sins, might live for righteousness—by whose stripes you were healed" (1 Pet. 2:24). Isaiah 53:5 was fulfilled in Christ's death, but it is a *reference to sin, not sickness*!

Just because Peter used the word "heal" does not mean he had physical sickness in mind. The context indicates that he is talking about sin, not sickness. Therefore, the word "heal" in 1 Peter 2 refers to healing from sin's spiritual sickness.

Lewis Sperry Chafer illustrates Peter's use of healing in I Peter 2 by pointing to Paul's use of riches in 2 Corinthians 8. He states, "He was made poor that others might be made rich (II Cor. 8:9), but none would assert that because of that truth, men have temporal riches provided for them in the death of Christ, which riches only await the faith that claims them. Reference to riches contemplates spiritual riches that wait on faith to claim them. In the same manner, healing by the stripes that Christ received is spiritual, or that of the soul, and not physical, or that of the body (Chafer, vol. III, p. 38).

To put it all succinctly, Isaiah 53:4, which refers to sickness, was fulfilled during Christ's life, not His death. Isaiah 53:5, which refers to sin, was fulfilled in Christ's death. Christ did not take care of sickness in His death no more than He solved the sin problem in His life. So, although Isaiah 53 is one of the outstanding chapters in the Bible on Christ's death, it does not teach that Christ died for sickness as He died for sin. Other topics covered in Isaiah 53 are not included in the atonement. Only a superficial treatment of that text sees sickness in that chapter and atonement in that passage and then assumes that sickness was involved in the atonement.

The Theological Issue There is a theological question involved in teaching healing in the atonement. Does sickness need atonement? Sin is a moral issue. Man disobeyed God. The penalty is death. Therefore, in the case of sin, an atonement was necessary. Christ provided that atonement by becoming our substitute to die for our sins, but sickness is not a moral issue. Sickness is not sin; it is the result of sin, the sin of Adam. People are not punished for sickness. The wages of disease is not death. The Bible nowhere teaches that sickness needs atonement. Christ did not become cancer that we might be forgiven malignancy.

Dr. Alva J. McClain, a past president of Grace Seminary in Winona Lake, Indiana, wrote a small booklet entitled, *Was Christ Punished for Our Disease?* (The very title clarifies the issue, doesn't it?). In it, he said, "The cause of this error seems to arise out of the confusion of two separate things, namely sin and disease. Sickness is not sin; it is rather the *result* of sin. We punish men for sinning but not for getting sick. Certainly, a man may become diseased through breaking the moral law, but in dealing with such a man, we separate sin from the disease. The laws of nations are far from perfect, but they do not punish men for being sick. Once we see this clearly, it is easy to find our way out of the confusion about healing and the atonement" (McClain, p. 7).

Having established that Christ did not become a substitute for sin, it needs to be added that there is a sense in which the death of Christ will ultimately eliminate all disease from the universe. The entrance of sin into the human family brought with it demon activity, degeneration, disease, and death. The whole earth is under a curse. Paul says, "The creation was subjected to futility ... the creation itself also will be delivered from the bondage of corruption into the glorious liberty of the children of God. We know that the whole creation groans and labors with birth pangs together until now" (Rom. 8:20-22). The work of Christ on the cross accomplished the reconciliation of all things to God (Col. 1:20). Satan was also defeated there (Col. 2:15). In a sense, all blessings come through the work of Christ on the cross (see "all" things in Rom. 8:32), but that does not mean that all the benefits of the cross are mine to enjoy now (for example, resurrection, and a glorified body), nor does it mean that Christ died as a substitute for all these things as He died as a substitute for sin. Healing is not a *right* established for the present through the atoning work of Christ.

Lockyer has stated it well. "Examining the assertion that there is something in sickness which needs atoning, it is not hard to discover the unscriptural character of such teaching. Healing is not an integral part of the gospel. Paul never included it in his proclamation of the Evangel. Nowhere does he associate the healing of the body with the cross. Atonement to the apostles was for sin, and sin only.... That there is healing in the atonement is only true in that all gifts and blessings come to us from the cross. 'He that spared not His Son but delivered Him up for us all, how shall He not with Him also freely give us all things' (Rom. 8:32). There are many blessings in the cross, the fullness of time for the enjoyment of which has not yet arrived. Deliverance from death is ours through the atonement, yet death is still there. The atonement covers the millennial age to come, as well as the age in which we presently live. Calvary removed the curse of sin, but this curse is still upon the whole creation, groaning to be delivered from such thralldom. As we cannot, therefore, claim in this age all that is included under the atonement of Christ, we cannot claim universal exception from sickness on the ground of the finished work of Christ" (Lockyer, pp. 17-19).

Did Christ Die For Sickness?

Summary: A careful study of the Scriptures related to the death of Christ indicates that Christ did not die to make believers healthy in this age but to make them holy.

The fact that Christ did not die for sickness does not necessarily mean that God does not heal. He could heal on some other basis (See the chapter, "Does God Heal Today?"). Even though healing is not in the atonement, Christ and the apostles healed in the New Testament, but misunderstanding the biblical teaching of the atonement has caused problems and pain.

Those who teach healing in the atonement misrepresent the biblical data and usually emphasize physical healing. The Great Commission is to preach Christ's death as the basis of the forgiveness of sins. Healing had no place in the Great Commission. The healing movement, however, elevates it to the place of primary importance. In most cases, healing receives most of their energy and effort. If evangelism is present at all, it only receives an equal footing at best. At worst, it gets no attention at all. If Bible teaching is present, it usually centers on healing. The healing movement does not—as a whole—have the biblical emphasis. It is out of balance at best! Christ died to redeem us and reconcile us to God. That should be our message and mission, our passion and proclamation.

More importantly, those who teach healing in the atonement have disappointed and disillusioned many sincere but sick saints. If Christ died for sickness as He died for sin when people trust Him for healing, it would have to be guaranteed, as is forgiveness, when faith in Christ is present, but hundreds and thousands have believed Christ died for illness as He died for iniquity and were not healed. As a result, they were first disappointed, then disillusioned, and some ended up in despair. Some have died.

Let me illustrate. In his book *Where Is God When It Hurts*, Philip Yancey says, "Someone told me just before I became a Christian that God would heal me. It seemed too good to be true, and I didn't know if I dared believe it. But seeing nothing in the Bible that contradicted it, I began to hope and then to believe. But my faith was shaky. And when Christians came along and said, "God doesn't heal everyone," or "Affliction is a cross we must bear," my faith would waiver. Then, last fall, it just seemed to die. I gave up believing God would heal me.

"At that point in my life, I knew I couldn't face spending the rest of my life in the wheelchair; knowing that God had the power to heal me but wouldn't (or so I thought) made me very bitter. I would read Isaiah 53 and 1 Peter 2:24 and accuse God of holding the promise of healing before me like a piece of meat before a starving dog. He tempted me, showing the potential but never quite allowing me to reach it. This, in turn, produced deep guilt feelings because from the Bible, I knew God was a loving God and answerable to no man. I had such a conflict within me that my mental health was vicarious and I thought of suicide many times.

"I began to take tranquilizers just to get through the day as my guilt and resentment built a higher and higher wall between God and me. About this time, I began having headaches and problems with my eyes. An ophthalmologist could find no physical reason.

Did Christ Die For Sickness?

"I was still praying because I knew God was alive, but I usually ended up crying and railing out at God. I'm afraid I experienced a lot of self-pity, which was very destructive. And over and over, I asked God why He wouldn't heal me when it so plainly said that healing was part of the redemptive plan" (Yancey, pp. 151-152).

Giving a person hope for healing is cruel when there is no basis for such hope in the Scripture. A correct understanding of the Word of God would have prevented such damaging despair.

Chapter 5

DOES THE GIFT OF HEALING EXIST TODAY?

The healing theology of the Protestant healing movement is Trinitarian. God the Father wills all believers to be well. God the Son died for sickness as He died for sin. God the Holy Spirit gives some the gift of healing today. The will of God the Father concerning physical healing and the work of God the Son on the cross have been discussed. The next question is, "Does the Holy Spirit give the gift of healing today?" The teaching of the faith healers is that the answer to that question is an emphatic "Yes."

For example, Bosworth wrote, "The age in which we live was intended by our heavenly Father to be the most miraculous of all the dispensations because it is the Miracle Worker's age, the Holy Spirit's dispensation. During this age, the great promise is that God will pour out the Holy Spirit, the Miracle Worker, upon all flesh. This is the only age in which the Miracle Worker would incarnate Himself; this is the only age in which the nine gifts of the Spirit—including the gifts of healing, healing, and miracles—were to be distributed to every man severally as He, the Holy Spirit, willed. Jesus declared that the works that He was doing would be continued and that even 'greater works' would be done by the Holy Spirit, the Miracle Worker, after He should have entered office during Christ's exaltation, which is during the

Spirit's dispensation" (Bosworth, p. 177).

Many have claimed to have the gift of physical healing. In his book *Seven Things You Should Know About Healing*, Kenneth Hagin says, "I have been awakened during the night and have realized that it was the Lord who awakened me. 'Lord, I don't know how to pray as I ought. You help me,' I have said. The Holy Spirit began to help me, and I began to pray aloud in other tongues, just lying there in bed beside my wife and never waking her. I have prayed that way thousands of times through these many years. Occasionally, when I have finished, I would have a vision. I would see my service the next night. I would see myself point to a person and I would hear myself say, 'I saw you last night in a vision in my room. You have.' .... (I would name what was wrong with them physically and I would tell them they were healed.) That was the gift of healings in operation. These people would be healed instantly; no one ever failed to be healed. You see, God had initiated something on His own. Such manifestations are signs of His presence and His power" (Hagin, p. 58).

Oral Roberts has pinpointed the presence of the gift of healing in his right hand. He has written, "My point of contact is God's presence that I often feel in my right hand. He spoke to me in an audible voice and said, 'Son, you have been faithful up to this hour. Now you shall feel My presence in your right hand; you shall detect the presence of demons and you shall have My power to cast them out.' Many people have been healed through this point of contact (Roberts, *Master Key to Healing*, p. 18).

Does The Gift Of Healing Exists Today?

These and others have claimed that the Holy Spirit has given them the spiritual gift of healing today. They are claiming more than having the gift of healing disease; they are claiming the ability to do miraculous things, like casting out demons, having supernatural knowledge, etc. What does the Bible say about healing and miracles? What was the purpose of healing and miracles in Bible times? Do these gifts exist today?

Miracles Confirm the Message

Christ In the New Testament, the gift of healing did not exist in isolation. It was exercised alongside other miracles. The first and foremost question is what was the purpose of the miraculous in the Bible?

In the case of Christ, His miracles confirmed His message. On the day of Pentecost, Peter said, "Men of Israel, hear these words: Jesus of Nazareth, the man attested by God to you by miracles, wonders, and signs, which God did through Him in your midst, as you yourselves also know" (Acts 2:22). The Greek word translated "attested" means "to show, declare, prove." The phrase "by God" means "from God." The order of the words in the Greek text suggests the translation, "Jesus of Nazareth, a man from God, attested (proven) to you by miracles." In other words, this verse says that the miracles of Jesus attested to the Jews and that He was from God. As Nicodemus said, "We know that You are a teacher come from God for no one can do these signs that You do unless God is with Him" (Jn. 3:2).

The word "attested" has been rendered "accredited." Jesus was accredited by miracles. I once heard an academic dean explain what accreditation meant to a college. He said, "The examining committee verified that we were doing what we said in the catalog we would do and that we met certain standards." Christ's miracles were His accrediting association. They affirmed and demonstrated that He was who He claimed to be.

The Apostles The Apostles performed miracles for the same reason Christ did, namely to confirm that their message was from God. Christ commissioned the apostles to preach the gospel to every creature, saying, "And these signs will follow those who believe: In My name, they will cast out demons; they will speak with new tongues; they will take up serpents; and if they drink anything deadly, it will by no means hurt them; they will lay hands on the sick, and they will recover" (Mk. 16:17-18). Mark adds, "And they went out and preached everywhere, the Lord working with them and confirming the word through the accompanying signs" (Mk. 16:20).

The text says, "These signs will follow those who believe." Does that mean that everyone who believes will perform miracles? Obviously not. There are no indications in the New Testament that every believer worked miracles. Nor should these words be taken to mean that every sign followed in every case. The reason Jesus said "those who believe" is because earlier He had rebuked them for their unbelief (Mk. 16:14).

What happened in the book of Acts? Acts records four of the five kinds of signs occurring. Peter, Phillip, and Paul cast out demons. Tongue speaking occurred on several occasions. Paul did not exactly take up a serpent, but one took up with him and he lived to tell the tale. Peter and Paul both healed the sick. However, there is nothing in Acts to indicate that anyone drank poison, but church history contains a well-known story concerning the apostle John. According to tradition, a fatal potion was prepared for him, but when he drank it, he was unhurt.

Paul said of his ministry, "Truly the signs of an apostle were accomplished among you with all perseverance, in signs and wonders and mighty deeds" (2 Cor. 12:12). If all believers were to perform miracles, they would not have served as a sign of apostleship.

These "signs of an apostle" have been called an "insignia" of apostleship. Charles Hodge put it like this. "The signs of an apostle were the insignia of the apostleship, those things which by divine appointment were made the evidence of a mission from God. When these were present, an obligation rested on all who witnessed them to acknowledge the authority of those who bore those insignias. When they were absent, it was, on the one hand, an act of sacrilege to claim the apostleship, and, on the other, an act of apostasy from God to admit its possession. To acknowledge the claims of those who said that they were apostles and were not was (and is) to turn from God to the creature, to receive as divine what was, in fact, human or Satanic. This is evidently Paul's view of the matter, as appears from [2 Cor.] 11:13-15 where he speaks of those who were the ministers of Satan and yet claimed to be the apostles of Christ" (Hodge, pp. 290-291).

The Sign Gifts have Ceased

There is evidence in the New Testament that the sign gifts ceased before the end of the apostolic age. Some of this evidence consists of logical inferences, while other bits of evidence are more direct. All the evidence together presents a compelling case.

Apostleship For example, there are no apostles today because no one today has the qualifications of an apostle. One of the requirements for being an apostle was to have seen the risen Christ. In Acts 1, when the apostles were contemplating replacing Judas, Peter said, "One of these must become a witness with us of His resurrection" (Acts 1:22). There is a debate as to whether they were right in replacing Judas, but there is no question that they understood that an apostle had to have seen Christ after the resurrection.

Paul said that. In 1 Corinthians 9:1, he says, "Am I not an apostle? Am I not free? Have I not seen Jesus Christ our Lord?" He refers to his encounter with the risen Christ on the road to Damascus. No one today has seen the resurrected Christ. Therefore, no one today is an apostle.

Another indication that there are no apostles today, nor can there be, is that apostles were the foundation, not the superstructure of the church. The book of Ephesians teaches that the church was "built on the foundation of the apostles and prophets" (Eph. 2:20). The apostles and prophets were the foundation of the church in that they came first and their preaching laid the foundation for it. The foundation is laid at the beginning of a building. It is not on the twenty-first floor! If the apostles and prophets were the foundation at the beginning of the church in the first century, the implication is that they do not exist in the twenty-first century. That's a safe assumption.

If apostles do not exist today, neither do the signs of apostleship!

Sign Gifts The book of Hebrews contains a statement clearly stating the purpose of the sign gifts and implying that they have ceased. It says, "How shall we escape if we neglect so great a salvation, which at the first began to be spoken by the Lord, and was confirmed to us by those who heard Him, God also bearing witness both with signs and wonders, with various miracles, and gifts of the Holy Spirit, according to His own will?" (Heb. 2:3-4).

This passage teaches that: 1) The Lord first spoke the message. 2) The message was confirmed to us, both writer and readers, by those who heard the Lord. 3) God also bore witness with signs. The question is, "Who performed the signs?" The answer is "Those who heard the Lord." The word "confirmed" is in the past tense (Greek: the aorist tense). In the Greek text, "bearing witness" is a present tense participle, which describes action contemporaneous with the main verb "was confirmed." In other words, "both the eyewitness testimony and the miraculous corroboration were past events. The verb tenses do not indicate that these things were still in the process of occurring" (Burdick, p. 38). The King James Version translates Hebrews 2:4, "God also bearing *them* witness." The word "them" is not in the Greek text, so the King James translators put it in italics, but the Greek construction indicates that they were correct in doing so.

The point of the passage is that God confirmed the messages to us by them—not to us by miraculous signs, but to us *by them who did supernatural things*. Why did those called "us" not perform the miracles? The sign gifts had ceased with those who heard the Lord (the apostles).

Hebrews 2 indicates that all the sign gifts have ceased. It specifically speaks of "signs and wonders, with various miracles, and gifts of the Holy Spirit" (Heb. 2:4).

Hoekema explained Hebrews 2 in more detail. He says, "According to this passage, the word of salvation was first spoken by the Lord Jesus Christ Himself. It was then confirmed to both the writer and the readers of this epistle by those who heard the Lord. 'Them that heard him' could designate either the apostles or a wider circle than the apostles; the reference to signs and wonders in the next verse, however, makes it rather likely that the apostles are here meant. The tense of the participle in verse 4, which is rendered "bearing witness," is present, indicating that the witness about to be described was a continuing one. How, now, did God bear witness with the apostles to the authenticity of the gospel message? By 'signs and wonders, and with divers miracles, and gifts of the Holy Ghost' (v. 4). The last word, translated *gifts*, means *distributions* (merismois); it clearly refers to the various gifts of the Holy Spirit, such as are described in 1 Corinthians 12, and undoubtedly includes glossolalia. The function, then, of all these special gifts or charismata of the Spirit is here described as one of confirmation: God continually bore witness with the apostles through these gifts and thereby confirmed the message of salvation to the second-generation readers of the Epistle to the Hebrews.

"From the passages just discussed, we learn that the purpose and function of the special miraculous gifts of the Spirit were to authenticate the apostles as true messengers from God and, thus, to confirm the gospel of salvation. This being the case, we can understand why these miraculous signs should be so much in evidence in apostolic times. But, this being the case, we can also understand why these miraculous signs should disappear when the apostles passed from the scene. If the miraculous signs were intended to authenticate the apostles, they would no longer be needed after the apostles had done their work.

"Our Pentecostal friends, however, like to say: These special miraculous gifts of the spirit are still needed today for the purpose of evangelism" (Hoekema, pp. 109-110).

The Gift of Healing Did miracles, including the gift of healing, actually cease in the apostolic age? Is there any indication in the New Testament that it happened, or is this all conjecture? In Acts 28, while on the Isle of Malta, Paul was bitten by a poisonous viper and should have died as a result, but did not (*cf.* Acts 28:1-6 with Mk. 16:18). He also healed many on the island (Acts 28:7-10). The year was AD 60.

Later, he landed in Rome, where he wrote the book of Philippians. In that book, he said Epaphroditus "was sick almost unto death; but God had mercy on him, and not only on him but on me also, lest I should have sorrow upon sorrow" (Phil. 2:27). Paul, who was able to heal on the way to Rome, could not heal

Epaphroditus at Rome when he first got sick. The year was AD 62.

Paul was released from his first Roman imprisonment and traveled again to Ephesus (1 Tim. 1:3). After he departed from Ephesus, Timothy, his representative there, developed stomach problems. In his first letter to his son in the faith, he told him to "no longer drink only water, but use a little wine for your stomach's sake and your frequent infirmities" (1 Tim. 5:23). That advice poses a number of problems for the advocates of the modern healing movement. If sickness is from Satan, why did Paul not tell Timothy to rebuke the devil? If it is always God's will to heal, why did not Paul counsel Timothy to pray for healing? If healing is in the atonement, why not have Timothy claim that which was his right? If Paul still had the power to heal, why did he not heal Timothy? Years before, while in Ephesus, where Timothy was when he received this letter, Paul had sent handkerchiefs and aprons from his body to the sick by which they were healed (Acts 19:11-12). Why didn't Paul send a handkerchief with his letter? The year was AD 63.

At the end of his life, Paul left Trophimus sick at Miletus (2 Tim. 4:20). Why did Paul not heal him before he left? The year was AD 67.

The conclusion is inescapable. The record reveals that Paul healed as late as AD 60, yet there is nothing recorded after that date to indicate that Paul continued to heal and, there are several instances to indicate that he no longer healed.

The sign gifts were never intended to continue throughout the church age. Nothing in the New Testament indicates that anyone would have these abilities after the apostles passed off the scene. There is evidence that the sign gifts ceased. God is not in the sign business today. With the completion of the New Testament canon, supernatural signs were no longer needed. The message of Christ and the apostles has been confirmed. The message is in written form. If a person will not believe God's Word, miracles will not do it either. Abraham told the rich man in hell that if his brothers did not hear Moses and the prophets, they would not be persuaded though one would be raised from the dead! (Lk. 16:31).

Healers Today

Well, if God is not working miracles and healing through healers today, how does one explain the claims of faith healers? There are several possible answers, all of which are true in some cases and together, probably explain as many as 99%, if not 100%, of the healers' "cases."

Fakery One possibility is that some of the so-called healings are nothing more than a false, fake, fraudulent recovery. Dr. William A. Nolen, in his book *Healing, a Doctor in Search of a Miracle*, tells of Christian healers in the Philippines who performed psychic surgery. He cites one case he calls "flagrant examples of fakery." He says, "A classic example involved a patient who had undergone a hip operation by a surgeon in the United States, presumably to fix a fracture. The woman had several screws and a metal plate in her hip, and these metallic objects, she believed, were causing her pain. Tony Agpaoa operated on her, removed the hardware and showed it to her. As soon as the operation was over, she was free of pain. Amazing! Wonderful! Miraculous—right? Sounds that way, certainly. Unfortunately for Tony Agpaoa, metallic objects showed up quite clearly on X-rays. Several months later, when her doctor in the United States took repeated X-rays, it was obvious that all the screws and the metal plates were still in her hip. The patient's pain relief had been psychogenic" (Nolen, p. 24).

In his magazine, *The New Day*, the Reverend W. V. Grant ran a full-color photo of Morris Kidd of Racine, Wisconsin. The caption read, "This Milwaukee Man Was Blind All of His Life. After Rev. Grant prayed, he saw for the first time." The truth, however, was that Mr. Kidd had not been blind all of his life. His sight had only deteriorated for a few years, but more importantly, he was just as blind after the prayer by Grant as he was before. His wife said that the photo and the caption were misleading. 'It was just a hoax.' She suggested that Grant should be 'put out of business for lying to people' ("Be Healed in the Name of God, an Expose of Rev. W. V. Grant," James Randi, *Free Inquiry*, Spring, 1986, vol. 6, no. 2, p. 11).

Evangelist Peter Popoff of Upland, California, claims, or at least gives the impression at his healing meetings, that the Holy Spirit gives him the names and diseases of sick people in the audience. He then calls out their names and illnesses and lays hands on them to heal them. A group named "The Committee for the Scientific Investigation of Religion" discovered that Popoff's wife and aids gathered the information from the audience in conversations before the service and from prayer request cards filled out there. Then Elizabeth, Popoff's wife, transmitted the information to Peter via a tiny receiver in his left ear.

When James Randi, the head of the committee, made their finds public on April 22, 1986, on the *Tonight Show*, starring Johnny Carson, Popoff acknowledged in an interview that it was true, but "said his wife supplied him with only about half the names. The other half I would pray and wait on the Lord, I'm not denying the divine" (*Los Angeles Times*, May 11, 1986, part II, p. 1).

By the way, the committee members also requested healing, giving false names and phony sicknesses. One pretender said Popoff prayed for his healing three times: as a bearded man suffering from alcoholism, as a clean-shaven balding man with arthritis, and wearing a dress and wig as a woman with uterine cancer, confined to a wheelchair. Randi said the ploy demonstrated that if God were informing Popoff, He was giving him wrong information (*Los Angeles Times*, loc. cit., p. 2).

Throughout the history of the healing movement, there have been cases of inaccurate reports. Years ago, Gaebelein said that in his book, *The Ministry of Healing*, A. J. Gordon cited the case of a boy who was miraculously healed of a double fracture of the arm. The healer was W. E. Boardman, who declared that the child's arm was miraculously healed and the next day was perfectly whole.

Dr. James Henry Lloyd of the University of Pennsylvania thoroughly investigated this case. In the "medical record" for

March 27, 1886, Dr. Lloyd published a letter from *the very child* who had become a physician.

"Dear Sir: The case you cite when robbed of all of its sensational surroundings, is as follows: the child was a spoiled youngster who would have his own way, and when he had a greenstick fracture of the forearm, and after having had it bandaged for several days, concluded that he would much prefer going without a splint. The splint was removed to please the spoiled child, and the arm was carefully adjusted in a sling. As a matter of course, the bone soon united as is customary in children, and, being only partially broken, all the sooner. This is the miracle! Some nurse or crank or religious enthusiast, ignorant of matters physiological and histological, evidently started the story and, unfortunately, my name—for I am the party—is being circulated in circles of faith and is given the sort of notoriety I did not crave. Very respectfully yours, Carl H. Reed" (Gaebelein, pp. 90-91).

Dr. George W. Peters, former professor of World Missions at Dallas Theological Seminary, documented a dramatic illustration of an inaccurate report. He studied firsthand the Indonesian revival in general and healing in particular. He interviewed people allegedly raised from the dead. He concluded that the people who were reportedly raised from the dead were never dead at all! He discovered that the word for "death" in their language may mean "unconsciousness, coma, or actual death." He concluded that based on their usage of the word death and their concept of death, they had only experienced resuscitations. According to our idea of death, no miracle actually happened. He explains all of this in detail in his book, *The Indonesian Revival* (Peters, pp. 80, 83).

Benjamin Franklin once said, "There are no greater liars than quacks—except for their patients." The imagination of their victims helps healers. They will say that they are healed when they know they are not. Some take pride in the ability to believe despite contrary evidence.

Remission There are also indications of the disease going into temporary remission and of patients calling it a cure. Dr. Nolen says, "Multiple sclerosis is a terrifying disease. No one knows what causes it or how to cure it. Hundreds of drugs alone or in combination have been used to treat the disease. None so far have been consistently helpful.

"In the short run, however, almost any treatment will seem to work. There are two reasons for this. First, the disease is cyclic; its symptoms may come and go. One day, a patient may be blind in his left eye; the next day, his vision may be normal. He may lose bladder control for three months, then regain it, have perfect control for a year, then lose control again. He may develop paralysis in his legs, which become so bad that he can get around only in a wheelchair; then, gradually, his strength may return so he can walk unaided.

"It is only by studying large groups of patients over long periods of time that an investigator can tell whether improvement in a patient with multiple sclerosis has been produced by the medicine under investigation or is just another remission for some unfathomable reason. So far, in all the studies that have been done, no one has found firm evidence that any medicine will cure multiple sclerosis.

"You will find, however, that because multiple sclerosis patients are always understandably looking for miracles, and because it is a cyclical disease and responsive to suggestion, it is one of the diseases charlatans like to treat. No matter what the nonsense the faker preaches or practices, he inevitably finds it easy to persuade his desperate victim he has been helped" (Nolen, pp. 76, 77, 79).

Dr. Nolen tells the story of an eighteen-year-old girl who doctors diagnosed as having multiple sclerosis. She attended a healing meeting and, as a result, felt that her gait had improved and her headaches had decreased in frequency and intensity. She was sure she had been cured and it would be only a matter of time until she was perfectly normal. The doctors were unable to find any real change in her muscular strength. Remission is not healing.

Another outspoken Christian surgeon has concluded, "We in medicine do, from time to time, come across unexplained phenomena that may appear to be spontaneous healings controverting natural laws. The disease of cancer particularly may manifest strange and even permanent remission—Lewis Thomas, of the Memorial Sloan/Kettering Cancer Center, mentions knowledge of several hundred such cases. But the remission occurs among Christians and non-Christians, with prayer and without prayer, and they represent a very small percentage of the people with cancer who have been prayed for" (*Christianity Today*, Nov. 25, 1983, p. 18).

Does The Gift Of Healing Exists Today?

In 1966, Drs. Tilden Everson and Warren Cole, a former professor of surgery at the University of Illinois and a former president of the American College of Surgeons, wrote *Spontaneous Regression of Cancer*. They documented 176 cases of cancer remission.

Psychosomatic Illness To appreciate what often happens in a healing meeting, one must understand the difference between an organic and functional disease. An organic disease is one in which there is an actual alteration in the body's tissues. A functional disease is one in which the problem is primarily in the mind. For example, a person may not be able to see; he would say he is blind, but there is nothing organically wrong with his eyes. This is a psychosomatic illness. We would say, "It's all in his head." The healings in the Bible were of organic disease. Jesus healed the blind, the deaf, and the lame; so did the apostles.

It is difficult, if not impossible, to document by an outside objective source that healers heal organic diseases today. Notice how many "miracles" are hidden, such as tumors, headaches, or backaches. One Christian surgeon has said, "But from my own experience as a physician, I must truthfully admit that among the thousands of patients I have treated, I have never observed an unequivocal incidence of intervention in the *physical realm*. Many have prayed for; many found healing, but not in ways that counteracted the laws governing physiology. No case I have personally treated would meet rigorous criteria for a supernatural miracle (*Christianity Today*, Nov. 25, 1983, p. 18, italics in the original article).

What undoubtedly has happened is the healing of a psychosomatic illness. What those kind of people needed was to be told they would be healed and to believe it would happen, but what happened was the healing of a psychosomatic illness, not an organic disease.

Are not at least some healings actual healings of an organic disease? In the first place, there are very, very few, if any, such cases. To my knowledge, no healings have been documented in which the patient had not received some medical treatment first. Thus, as strange as it may sound, some "faith healings" are the result of doctors and medicine. Many, and probably most, patients who visit the healer's line have first been to the doctor's office, where they received treatment and medicine. When the healing took place, the healer, and not the doctor, received the credit.

Dr. Nolen tells of one such case. A man claimed to have been cured of prostate cancer by Kathryn Kuhlman. He sent Dr. Nolen a thorough report of his case. What Dr. Nolen discovered was that the man had had extensive treatment of his disease with surgery, radiation, and hormones. Dr. Nolen contends that prostate cancer is frequently responsive to hormone therapy, and even if it spreads, it is highly responsive to radiation therapy. The man who claimed to have been cured at a Kathryn Kuhlman meeting had received sufficient medical treatment to have been healed. Dr. Nolen concluded, "If Miss Kuhlman had to rely on this case to prove that the Holy Spirit 'cured' cancer through her, she would be in very desperate straits" (Nolen, pp. 100-101).

Does The Gift Of Healing Exists Today?

Satan Finally, even if it could be demonstrated that a particular healing was supernatural, which is doubtful, it does not necessarily follow that God did it. Satan has the power to perform miracles. By the power of God, Aaron cast out a rod before Pharaoh and it supernaturally became a serpent (Ex. 7:9-10). Pharaoh's magicians duplicated that fete, except Aaron's rod swallowed up their rods (Ex. 7:11-12). By whose power did Pharaoh's henchmen perform that miracle? Certainly not God's.

The second beast of Revelation 13 is said to have the power to perform great signs (Rev. 13:11-14). No doubt, this individual will work miracles by the power of Satan (2 Thess. 2:9). The same Greek words used of Christ and the apostles when they healed are used of Satan in 2 Thessalonians 2 and Revelation 13.

These references are not teaching that Satan heals today, but the fact that he did it in the past and will do it again in the future proves he can heal. We also know that one of the devil's devices is to imitate God, even to the point of disguising himself as an angel of light (2 Cor. 11:13-15). Dr. John MacArthur, in his book *The Charismatics*, states, "Satan has always helped people in his domain by means of counterfeit healings. Raphael Gasson, the former spiritualist medium who was converted to Christ, said, 'There are many, many spiritualists today who are endowed with this remarkable gift of power by Satan, and I myself, having been used in this way, can testify to having witnessed miraculous healings taking place at 'healing meetings' in spiritualism" (MacArthur, p. 135).

No Proof In spite of the grandiose claims of faith healers, it is difficult, if not impossible, to document their supernatural healings of an organic disease. This has been true throughout the history of the movement. Many years ago, a committee of eleven ministers of various denominations, eight Christian physicians, three university professors, and a lawyer investigated the results of a healing meeting conducted by C. S. Price in Vancouver, British Columbia, conducted by C. S. Price. After three months of detailed follow-up, they found that of the 350 people who professed to have been healed, they could not detect any physical change in the symptoms or in the conditions of 301. Furthermore, thirty-nine died within six months of the crusade; five became insane; and five others, suffering from various nervous disorders, apparently had been cured (Boggs, who cites A. C. Gaebelein, p. 28).

More recently, Dr. William A. Nolen, a noted Minnesota surgeon, investigated apparent healings in a Minneapolis Kathryn Kuhlman meeting. He had her permission and cooperation. During the healing service, as people who had "claimed a cure" came off the stage, two legal secretaries wrote down the names, addresses, phone numbers, and diseases of all who said they would help in a follow-up study. Eighty-two names were recorded. Later, letters were sent to all on the list, inviting them to a meeting to tell about their experience. Twenty-three showed up. After interviewing them, Dr. Nolen concluded, "In talking to these patients, I tried to be as honest, understanding, and objective as possible. The only thing I refused to dispense with—couldn't have dispensed with even if I had tried—were my medical knowledge and my common sense. I listened carefully to everything they told me and followed up every lead, which might even remotely have led to a confirmation of a miracle. When I had done all of this, I was led to an inescapable conclusion: none of the patients who had returned to Minneapolis to reaffirm the cures they claimed at the miracle service had, in fact, been miraculously cured of anything, either by Kathryn Kuhlman or the Holy Spirit" (Nolen, p. 90).

None of those who had claimed a cancer cure at the time of the service returned to reaffirm their cure, so Dr. Nolen wrote to everyone on his list who, at the time of the meeting, had claimed a cure for a malignancy. He called or visited those who did not respond. From that study, he concluded, "The more I learned of the result of Kathryn Kuhlman's miracle service, the more doubtful I became that any good she was doing could possibly outweigh the misery she was causing" (Nolen, p. 99).

Dr. Nolen then wrote Kathryn Kuhlman personally to ask for a list of patients she had cured so he could check on them. She sent him sixteen names, addresses, phone numbers, and diagnoses. Upon investigation of those, including six claiming a cancer cure, he was unable to document a bona fide cure of an organic disease.

Furthermore, he looked through hundreds of volumes for a year and a half to find "adequate documented examples of cures that could not be reasonably explained except in terms of miraculous powers." The results: "I couldn't find one such case" (Nolen, p. 265).

He personally tracked down twenty-three of the most promising leads he could find of people who had been healed by a healer who had not necessarily had a national reputation. He either called or visited the healer and the healed and talked with both at length. The results? "There were no miracles to be found" (Nolen, p. 268).

Ultimately, Dr. Nolen was forced to conclude, "Search the literature as I have and you will find no documented cures by healers of gallstones, heart disease, cancer, or any other serious organic disease. Certainly, you will find patients temporarily relieved of their upset stomachs, their chest pains, their breathing problems, and you will find healers and believers who will interpret this interruption of symptoms as evidence that the disease is cured, but when you track the patient down and find out what happened, you will always find the 'cure' to have been purely symptomatic and transient. The underlying disease remains" (Nolen, p. 293).

Summary: Miracles, including healings, were performed in biblical times to confirm the message, but there is evidence that sign gifts have ceased and there is little or no evidence that healers heal organic diseases today.

Claiming to heal and verifying a bona fide cure of an organic disease are two different things. It is possible that the healer believed healing occurred, and there is no doubt some have claimed to be healed, but proving such claims by an objective observer is difficult, if not impossible.

Does The Gift Of Healing Exists Today?

Perhaps the one thing healers do actually heal is psychosomatic illness. Keep in mind that many medical authorities have said that as high as 75% of people's ailments are mental. The symptoms of people with neurotic ailments will disappear if they believe they have been operated on by a man who can heal. The other supposed "cures" are possibly either: 1) a remission of a cyclical disease; 2) the "healing" of a self-limited disease (that is, a case of the body healing itself, as in the common cold); or 3) a cure that was actually brought about by medical treatment.

Two issues need to be clarified. While I am highly skeptical of divine healers, I believe in divine healing. See the chapter below, "Does God Heal Today?"

While the gift of healing may not exist today, there are gifted men today. Paul taught, "And He Himself gave some to be apostles, some prophets, some evangelists, and some pastors and teachers, for the equipping of the saints for the work of the ministry, for the edifying of the body of Christ, till we all come to the unity of the faith and the knowledge of the Son of God, to a perfect man, to the measure of the stature of the fullness of Christ; that we should no longer be children, tossed to and fro and carried about with every wind of doctrine, by the trickery of men, in the cunning craftiness by which they lie in wait to deceive, but, speaking the truth in love, may grow up in all things into Him who is the head—Christ—from whom the whole body, joined and knit together by what every joint supplies, according to the effective working by which every part does its share, causes growth of the body for the edifying of itself in love" (Eph. 4:11-16).

These gifted men are not healers; they are evangelists, exhorters, pastors, and preachers. Their ministry is not touching the body but touching the mind. They produce stability in belief and behavior, not instability emotionally and spiritually. Don't be "blown away" by the false and the fake. Be stabilized by the truth in love.

Chapter 6

DOES YOUR HEALING DEPEND ON YOUR FAITH?

According to faith healers, the critical condition for receiving divine healing is faith on the part of the sick person. However powerful or successful the healer has been in other cases, the basis for healing in each case is the faith of the person with the illness.

Deliverance evangelists quote Scripture to demonstrate that faith is the key to healing. Jesus Himself said, "Have faith in God. For assuredly, I say to you, whoever says to this mountain, 'Be removed and be cast into the sea,' and does not doubt in his heart but believes that those things he says will come to pass, he will have whatever he says. Therefore, I say to you, 'Whatever you ask when you pray, believe that you receive them and you will have them'" (Mk. 11:22-24). James said, "And the prayer of faith will save the sick." (Jas. 5:15).

Some go so far as to insist that when people say they believe and claim their healing, they are healed, but the healing has not been *manifested* yet. So, people with an obvious illness can say, "I'm healed," and it's just not been evidenced yet to those who are watching. They have been told and taught that they must believe no matter what they see or feel.

Bosworth put it like this. "To the extent that we base faith on our improvement, or are affected by our symptoms, or by what we see or feel instead of by the Word of God alone, just to that extent ours is not real faith. To be occupied with what we see or feel is to reverse the condition God laid down for us to follow. 'Everyone who looketh at it shall live' simply means that everyone who, like Abraham, so occupies himself with God's promise that he is no longer affected by symptoms 'shall recover.' It means the Word of God (not what we see or feel) shall be the basis of our faith" (Bosworth, p. 106).

Whether or not a particular healer goes to that extreme, faith remains the indispensable condition for healing in the healing theology of the healing movement. Kenneth Hagin, speaking to the faithless in a sermon, declared, "You can lay your hands on folks like that [i.e., faithless folks] until you've worn every hair off the top of their head, and all you're going to get out of it will be a bald head" (Harrell, p. 86). (Kathryn Kuhlman was the exception. She believed that God healed believers and unbelievers.)

Is the faith of the sick person the key to faith healing? When a person fails to be healed in a healing meeting, the standard explanation is that the person did not have enough faith. Is that correct? To answer that question, consider what the Scripture says about the relationship between faith and healing.

Some had Faith and were Healed

Matthew 9 An examination of the Scriptural examples of healing indicates that some had faith and, as a result, were healed. Matthew 9 records two typical examples.

Does Your Healing Depend On Your Faith?

An unidentified woman had suffered from hemorrhaging for twelve years. From a Jewish point of view, this was a horrible and humiliating disease because the Mosaic Law declared such a person ceremonially unclean (Lev. 15:25-27). Everything and everyone she touched, according to Leviticus, was infected by her uncleanness. Consequently, she was isolated from the worship of God and the fellowship with other people. This woman had been like that for twelve years!

The woman with the issue of blood had either heard that Christ was healing or she had seen Him do it. She clearly believed He could heal her and conceived of just touching His garment to be healed. Slipping through the crowd (If they had known about her problem, they would have screamed, "Unclean!"), she came behind Jesus and touched the hem of His garment.

Spurgeon says, "Great fear kept her from facing Him. Great faith led her to believe that a touch of His robe *behind Him* would cure her. She was ignorant enough to think that healing went from Him unconsciously, yet her faith lived despite her ignorance and triumphed despite her bashfulness. Her idea was to make a dash for it and steal a cure" (Spurgeon, p. 61).

The moment she touched Jesus' garment, He turned, looked at her and said, "Be of good cheer, daughter; your faith has made you well" (Mt. 9:22b). Matthew adds, "And the woman was made well from that hour" (Mt. 9:22c). Her finger touched His garment, her faith touched His heart, and she was healed.

Later in Matthew 9, another healing based on the faith of a sick person is recorded. Two sightless men had become companions.

They heard Jesus was healing, found Him, followed Him, and pleaded with Him: "Son of David, have mercy on us!" (Mt. 9:27). They may have been blind, but they could see who Jesus was, the Son of David, the promised Messiah. This is the first time anyone in the Gospel of Matthew addressed Jesus as the Son of David.

Jesus did not immediately respond. They persisted. When Jesus entered a house, they followed and pleaded again. This time, He asked: "Do you believe that I am able to do this?" (Mt. 9:28b). He did not inquire about their eyes, only about their faith. They could not see, but they did believe. They immediately responded, "Yes, Lord" (Mt. 9:28c). Moments before, they addressed Him as the Son of David. Now they called Him "Lord."

These two blind men touched Jesus with their faith. He touched their eyes, saying, "According to your faith, let it be to you" (Mt. 9:29). Matthew reports, "And their eyes were opened" (Mt. 9:30). They both saw. In one moment, two received sight.

Jesus opened their eyes and desired that they should close their mouths. He instructed them to tell no one (Mt. 9:30). He was not seeking fame. He did not want this miracle known, at least not at this moment. They could not contain themselves, however. They spread the news about Him throughout the country (Mt. 9:31).

These are but two of the examples of Christ healing someone who had faith. One was the case of a woman. The other was an incident involving two men. All had serious physical problems.

Acts 14 Other examples appear on the pages of the New Testament. For instance, in Acts 14, Paul encountered a deformed, crippled man who had never walked. Luke records, "And in Lystra a certain man without strength in his feet was sitting, a cripple from his mother's womb, who had never walked" (Acts 14:8). Paul told him to "stand up straight on your feet!" (Acts 14:10). Alexander points out that the command to "stand up straight" implies that this cripple was also bent over or otherwise deformed (Alexander, p. 115). At any rate, the man had never walked; he was helpless. Congenital infirmities of this kind were commonly regarded as incurable; the man was hopeless.

Paul's preaching captured this hopeless, helpless man. As he listened, hope was born in his bosom; faith was formed in his soul. His attention was firmly fixed on the announcer of the good news he was hearing. "Observing him intently," Paul was "seeing that he had faith to be healed" (Acts 14:9). So, he "said with a loud voice, 'Stand up straight on your feet!'" (Acts 14:10). The cripple leaped and walked (Acts 14:10). He had faith and now he had feet that functioned.

Some did not have Faith and were Healed

No Faith On the other hand, some did not exercise faith, yet they were healed. On numerous occasions, Jesus healed, but nothing was said about the faith of the healed person. Perhaps it could be argued that the individuals had faith, but that fact is not recorded. That is an argument for silence, which is weak at best. It is just as logical to conclude that faith was not required of these sick people. For example, Jesus healed a demon-possessed mute, but nothing is said concerning the mute having faith (Mt. 9:32-33).

Indeed, he couldn't hear! Other examples could be cited (2 Kings 5; Job 42:10; Dan. 4; Mt. 12:9-14,22; Mk. 7:31-37; 8:22-26; Lk. 14:1-4; 22:47-51; Jn. 5:1-9, 9:1-7; Acts 5:12-16; 19:11-12; 28:8-9).

Others had Faith Then, there are those cases where the sick person did not have faith, but someone else did! Once, Jesus was speaking in a house packed with people. The place was so crowded no one could even get near the door (Mk. 2:1-2). Four friends of a paralytic brought him to Jesus to be healed. When they could not get to Him because of the crowd, they lowered him through the roof. Mark says, "When Jesus saw *their* faith, He not only healed the paralytic, He forgave him! (Mk. 2:3-5, italics added). This kind of healing took place on more than one occasion (Mt. 8:5-13; 15:21-28; Mk. 9:14-29; Jn. 4:46-54).

In absentia In some cases, the healing was in absentia; the sick person was not in the presence of Jesus when the healing occurred. In those cases, evidently, the healing was not the result of the sick person's faith but the response of Jesus to the request of someone else (Mt. 8:5-13; 15:21-28; Jn. 4:46-54).

In studying the place of faith in Christ's healing ministry, Boggs concluded, "That faith was an important factor in Jesus' cures of the sick no one will question. When faith was absent, this apparently, at times, placed a limitation upon even Jesus' ability to heal. Because of the unbelief of people in Nazareth, "he could do no mighty work there, except that he laid his hands upon a few sick people and healed them." (Mark 6:5.) Nevertheless, the nature and place of faith in Jesus' healing ministry is not nearly so

Does Your Healing Depend On Your Faith?

plain as is often supposed, and much damage has been done by the faith healers who fail to note how Jesus varied His methods to suit the needs of His patients.

"Out of the twenty instances of healing under consideration, in eight cases, the sick person seemed to have some sort of faith before the cure.

"But it should not be supposed that Jesus never healed without this antecedent faith. On the contrary, there are three cases where it was almost certainly lacking. The man who had been ill for thirty-eight years had no antecedent faith and, in fact, did not even know who Jesus was when the Jewish officials questioned him following his cure. Afterward, Jesus found him in the Temple and gave him more instruction about the cause of his sickness and the way to prevent a recurrence (John 5:2-15). If faith entered the picture at all in this case, it followed the cure and was induced by it. Almost certainly, there was no antecedent faith operative in the healing of the woman who had been bent over for eighteen years (Luke 13:12), and this is also generally interpreted to be the case with the woman cured of a flow of blood (Mark 5:25-34).

"In three other cases, it is not the sick person who has the faith, but his friends or relatives. In the case of the paralytic let down through the roof by four friends, Mark records that "when Jesus saw *their* faith" (Mark 2:5), He proceeded to heal him. The faith of the Syro-Phoenician mother was instrumental in the cure of her daughter, who was at a distance and never even saw Jesus. (Mark 7:24-30.) Again, Jesus commended a centurion for his faith (Matthew 8:5-10), which was instrumental in the healing of his slave, who was also some distance from Jesus and had no direct contact with Him.

"From all of this, the difficulty of defining precisely the role, or faith in the healing ministry of Jesus may be seen" (Boggs, pp. 61-63).

Some had Faith and were not Healed

Someone might argue that in the cases of another having faith, at least faith was exercised. Are there cases of someone having faith and not receiving healing? The answer is "Yes." Paul had a thorn in the flesh for which he pleaded with the Lord three times that it might be removed (2 Cor. 12:7, 9). Granted, the text does not say Paul did or did not have faith, but is there any doubt that *Paul*, the apostle of faith, believed God when he prayed? Yet, he was not healed.

The passage that relates Paul's problem with the thorn also records Paul's visit to the third heaven (2 Cor. 12:2-5; Commentators agree that Paul is speaking of himself and uses the third person to avoid the charge of boasting). How far apart were the two events? Lenski suggests Paul does not say when this thorn was first inflicted on him. All that one may surmise is that it may well have happened a short time after the visit to paradise because the two are such opposites, and Paul narrates them together. Then Paul made three efforts that urged the Lord to rid him of the plague (Lenski, p. 1302).

Does Your Healing Depend On Your Faith?

If Paul had just returned from heaven, would he have had difficulty believing that God would and could heal? Even if the two events were not close in time, just to have had the experience of visiting heaven would have given Paul faith to believe that God would remove his thorn.

Paul is not the only one who had faith and was not delivered. Hebrews 11 is the "hall of fame" of faith. The writer to the Hebrews points to a whole host of men and women who had faith and received what they believed God would do (see esp. Heb. 11:32-35a), but he also says that there were heroes of the faith who had faith and were *not* delivered (Heb. 11:35b-40). Westcott, calling this catalog "the victorious sufferings of faith," says, "The record of the open triumphs of faith is followed by the record of its inward victories in unconquered and outwardly unrewarded endurance" (Westcott, p. 379).

Summary: Healing in the Bible did not always depend on the sick person's faith.

It ought to be obvious that healing did not always depend on the faith of the person needing a divine touch because people were raised from the dead! (1 Kings 17:17-24; 2 Kings 4:18-37; 13:20-21; Mt. 9:18-26; Lk. 7:11-17; Jn. 11:1-44; Acts 9:36-43; 20:9-12).

The conclusive proof is in Matthew 17. Jesus sent the disciples to preach and gave them the power to heal (Mt. 10:1-8). In Matthew 17, the father of an epileptic who had suffered severely came to Christ complaining that the disciples could not cure his son (Mt. 17:14-16). After Jesus exorcized the child and he was cured, the disciples asked, "Why could we not cast him out?" (Mt. 17:19). The Lord told His disciples, whom He had given the power to heal, that they could not heal in this case, "Because of *your* unbelief" (Mt. 17:20, italics added)! Healing in the Bible did not always depend on the sick person's faith. No one has the right to tell anyone that he or she was not healed because of a lack of faith on his part. To do so is untrue and uncharitable; it's downright cruel.

It is wrong to suggest, as Job's so-called friends did that sickness is a sure sign of not being right with God, as in not claiming healing by faith.

Boggs wrote, "Let neither the sick nor the well person forget that at the heart of our Christian religion is a cross. A few days before his fatal cerebral hemorrhage, Dr. Edmond Wilie was visiting with us in our living room. He was a retired Presbyterian minister who had served important churches in Montclair, New Jersey, and New York City. He had learned of my book of faith healing and had come over to express empathetic agreement with its thesis that God does not always reward true faith with bodily healing. He had discovered in his own long experience as a Christian pastor that it is not always the Father's will to remove the cup of suffering. He told us he had tried to set forth his Christian insight on a Christmas card we would soon receive. A few days before we received the card, Dr. Wilie was fatally stricken and called to his eternal home, so when the card finally arrived, it meant all the more to us. His message read, 'There is a faith greater than that of answered prayer: that is the faith of the

Does Your Healing Depend On Your Faith?

Man of the cross who was born at Christmas…. That greater faith I wish for you.' I can do no better than to echo Dr. Wilie's wish to my readers. Discovered on the wall of a Denver hospital were these words in which this same Christian message found eloquent expression:

> "The cry of man's anguish went up unto God,
> 'Lord, take away pain!
> The shadow that darkens the world Thou hast made; the close-coiling chain that strangles the heart; the burden that weighs on the wings that would soar—Lord, take away pain from the world Thou hast made, that it love Thee the more!'
>
> Then answered the Lord to the cry of His world:
> 'Shall I take away pain,
> And with it, the power of the soul to endure, Made strong by the strain?
> Shall I take away pity that knits heart to heart and sacrifice high?
> Will ye lose all your heroes that lift from the fire White brows to the sky?
> Shall I take away the love that redeems with a price and smiles at its loss?
> Can ye spare from your lives that would climb unto mine The Christ on His cross?"
>
> (Boggs, pp. 184-185).

Chapter 7

DOES GOD HEAL TODAY?

In biblical times, God supernaturally healed. Some claim He continues to do so today. Does He? If He does, how does He do it?

The healing movement within Protestant Christianity teaches that since all sickness is from Satan, it is always God's will to heal, and that Christ died for sickness, any time anyone exercises faith, God will heal them. The Scriptures do not support such a theology.

The question, then, becomes, does God heal today apart from healers and healing lines? Does God sanction doctors and drugs? Does He ever heal today without physicians and pills? Would God approve a combination of pills and prayer?

On one extreme are those who claim that God heals and that only God should heal. Therefore, according to them, it is wrong, and even wicked, to see a doctor. Throughout the history of the healing movement, some have taken the extreme position that doctors and drugs should not be used. John Alexander Dowie once wrote an article entitled "Doctors, Drugs and Devils," where he placed all three in the same category!

More recently, Dr. Hobart E. Freeman, a man with a doctorate in theology from Grace Theological Seminary in Winona Lake, Indiana, said, "To claim healing for the body and then to continue to take medicine is not following our faith with the corresponding action. One should settle the matter beforehand; if we have faith that God will keep His word and heal us, we will not need to keep our medicines and remedies around 'just in case.' If we feel the need of anything in addition to faith, then we do not have faith to be healed. One should not 'try' divine healing as one means of 'cure,' which we think sometimes works for some people and just might work for us. This is a popular misconception of the Scriptural doctrine of healing through faith and always results in failure. When genuine faith is present, it alone will be sufficient, for it will take the place of medicine and other aids" (Freeman, p. 11).

On the other extreme are those who insist that God does not heal today. According to their view, doctors and medicine are the only hope for the ill.

Does God heal today, and if so, how? What should a Christian do when he is sick? Should he see a doctor? Should he take medication? Should he pray? Should he do one and not the other, or should he do all of the above?

God Heals through Doctors

Doctors According to the Scripture, what should Christians' attitudes and practices concerning doctors and medicine be? Two passages are often cited as support for the view that doctors should not be used: one in the Old Testament and one in the New Testament.

Asa, a king in the Northern Kingdom, "became diseased in his feet." When the malady grew "very severe," instead of seeking the Lord, he sought physicians (2 Chron. 16:12). The author of Chronicles says, "So he rested with his fathers" (2 Chron. 16:13). This passage has been interpreted to mean that Asa died because he went to doctors and, therefore, believers should not go to physicians. Does this passage teach that Asa died because he sought a physician?

No! Keil, the famous Old Testament commentator, calls what Asa did "superstitious trust in the physician." He points out that the Hebrew construction used here is the same as the one used of seeking the help of idols, citing, among other passages, 1 Chronicles 10:13-14 where it is recorded that Saul died ... "because he consulted a medium for guidance but he did not inquire of the Lord; therefore He killed him." Keil concludes, "Consequently, it is not the mere inquiring of the physician which is here censured, but only the godless manner in which Asa trusted in the physicians" (Keil, p. 370). God did not kill Asa because he simply went to see a doctor. God Himself instructed Israel to do what was tantamount to visiting a physician (Deut. 24:8). Asa sought godless, ignorant quacks *instead* of the Lord. He shut God out of his life and his illness. For that, the Lord terminated his life.

The other passage that is sometimes used to teach that one should not seek medical help is in the New Testament. A woman who had hemorrhaged for twelve years is said to have "suffered many things from many physicians." She even spent all of her money seeking doctors but did not get any better, but only "grew worse" (Mk. 5:25-26). She is not the only person who has had that experience then or now!

Is Mark saying, "Do not ever see a doctor"? No. He only points out that the doctors this woman saw were powerless to heal her. Christ, by contrast, healed her with a touch. Luke, himself a physician, also recorded this incident. If she was to be blamed for seeing so many doctors, surely he would have been interested in that and would have said so, but rather than say anything like that, he states that she spent all of her livelihood on physicians and "could not be healed by any" (Lk. 8:43).

There is no doubt that Christians should go to doctors. No less than Jesus Christ Himself said, "Those who are well have no need of a physician, but those who are sick" (Mt. 9:12).

Medication What about medication? Does God sanction the use of aspirin, cortisone, and penicillin? The answer is "Yes." Christ's statement concerning doctors implies the use of medicine. Would He say, "Go see a doctor, but don't use their medicine"? Paul told Timothy, "No longer drink only water, but use a little wine for your stomach's sake and your frequent infirmities" (1 Tim. 5:23). Paul's advice is tantamount to telling Timothy to take medicine. Wuest says, "Wine was one of the chief remedial agents of those times when the science of medicine was in its infancy among Greek physicians. We must remind ourselves that Paul was speaking of wine as medicine here, not as a beverage" (Wuest, p. 88).

Another Greek professor put it like this. "In that day, wine was employed as a medicinal agent for many ailments. This has been true in medical practice until very recent times. Water was unsafe to drink in many parts of the world, and yet Timothy apparently was refraining from any use of the common beverage, wine.... Paul urges that the medicinal purpose is valid and should not be avoided when his health calls for it (Kent, pp. 187-188). Hiebert, also a Greek professor, concurs, saying, "The purpose of Paul's counsel was hygienic" (Hiebert, p. 105).

There is not one statement in the Scripture that even so much as hints that believers should not use doctors or drugs. On the contrary, Christ and Paul acknowledged the use of medicine. Just as eating, exercising, brushing your teeth, brushing your hair, and washing with soap are aids to good health, so is the proper use of medication and medical knowledge. If it is legitimate to eat food to build up the body so it can fight germs, which reside in everyone, why not take drugs that directly kill germs and disease?

Means In the final analysis, isn't it God who heals through the physician and pills? Does not God use means, even when He does the work? For example, when the children of Israel came to Marah, they could not drink the water because it was bitter. Moses cried out to the Lord and the Lord showed him a tree to cast into the bitter waters to make them sweet (Ex. 15:22-26). God healed the waters, but He used means. Likewise, God heals people (Ex. 15:26) by using the means of modern medicine.

Calvin speaks "of God working in and through 'the ordinary course of nature' in His work of providence. Among those ordinary works of providence are winds (Heb. 1:7), thunder, lightning, earthquakes (Ps. 29:3, 7-8), and "healing the diseases of some who are almost dead" (Calvin, *Institutes*, Book 1, ch. 5, para. 5).

That does not mean that the doctor is aware that he is the instrument of divine providence. Nevertheless, as Benjamin Franklin has said, "God heals and the doctor takes the fee."

On the other hand, to go to the extreme of teaching that Christians should not see a doctor has been and can be tragic. Hobart Freeman, the man with a doctorate in theology, who was quoted at the beginning of this chapter, is a classic case. He not only received a doctorate from Grace Seminary, but he also taught Hebrew there. However, in 1963, he was fired because of his doctrinal views. He began a ministry called "The Glory Barn." He preached to as many as 2,000 in his church. His disciples established churches in twenty-one other states and eight foreign countries. Freeman taught his followers to shun hospitals, doctors, and medicine. In 1983, the *Fort Wayne News-Sentinel* documented eighty-eight deaths from treatable illnesses and injuries in eleven states over eleven years because of Freeman's teachings.

God Heals through Elders

God not only heals through doctors, He also heals through elders! In the case of the physician, He uses their pills; in the case of elders, He uses their prayers. Just as the physician and his pills can apply in certain situations, so the elders and their prayers can only apply in certain cases. James explains when to call the elders.

James 5:14-20 has been abused more than it has been appropriately used. The Roman Catholic Church uses it to justify their administering the last rites to people just before they die, but the sick person in James 5 is supposed to live! Pentecostals and charismatics quote this passage to verify healing services, but the passage teaches that elders are to go to the sick person's home, not that the sick person is to go to church. Some dispensationalists relegate James 5 just to Jews, but the Jews in the book of James were Christians (Jas. 2:1). Then, some attempt to apply the instructions of James 5 to all who are sick. That is not what James intended.

The Sickness James 5:14-20 does not discuss all sickness regardless of its origin. It is dealing with sickness *due to sin*. James 5:15 links this sickness with sin. The problem is the verse sounds as if the person is deathly sick, but he may or may not have sinned. It says, "If he has committed sins." How do we know James 5 is talking about sickness due to sin?

In the first place, the context of the book naturally leads to that conclusion. The subject of James is trials. He begins the epistle probing that subject and concludes the book by dealing with the same thing (Jas. 1:2, 5:13, also 1:5 and 5:13). There is no doubt that the recipients of James were experiencing trials, both from without their assembly and from within it. Their wages were being withheld (Jas. 5:4), and they were being hauled into court (Jas. 2:6). They were also fighting among themselves (Jas. 4:1).

It can be argued that this book is designed to teach readers how to learn from their trials. James 1:19-20 is the key to the Book. James says, "Therefore my beloved brethren, let everyone be swift to hear, slow to speak, slow to wrath, for the wrath of man does not produce the righteousness of God" (Jas. 1:19-20). James 1:19 supplies the outline for the body of the book. "Be swift to hear," which is immediately defined as not just hearing but heeding the Word, is covered in James 1:21-2:26. "Be slow to speak" is the second section (Jas. 3:1-18). "Be slow to wrath" (Greek: "anger") is the essence of James 4:1-5:12. In other words, if believers respond appropriately to trials (Jas. 1:19), they will learn from them, that is, the practical righteousness of God will be worked out in their life (Jas. 1:20).

What if believers do not respond appropriately? Then they could become physically ill (1 Cor. 11:30). Hence, the book of James appropriately ends with a discussion of sickness due to sin.

The immediate context reinforces the conclusion that the last paragraph of James discusses sickness due to sin. James 4:1-5:12 is a unit. James charges that believers who fight have left God out of their lives (Jas. 4:1-10). Related to that is judging (Jas. 4:11-12), making plans without considering God (Jas. 4:13-17), and, in the case of unbelievers, leaving God out altogether (Jas. 5:1-6). When unbelievers, who totally leave God out of their lives, oppress believers, believers should not forget God themselves and grow impatient, grumble, and swear (Jas. 5:7-12). Thus, the context immediately preceding James 5:14-20 pictures Christians not responding well to the pressures and stresses of their lives. They were fighting among themselves (Jas. 4:1-10), judging one another (Jas. 4:11-12), making business plans without considering the will of God (Jas. 4:13-17), being impatient (Jas. 4:7), grumbling (Jas. 5:9) and swearing (Jas. 5:12). Their sins made them sick.

Therefore, James concludes by telling them what to do with sickness due to sin.

Does not James 5:15 say "if"? Does not that mean "maybe"? (The Greek construction here is a third-class condition, which usually means something like "maybe.") In John 14:3, however, Jesus said, "And if (a third-class condition in Greek) I go and prepare a place for you, I will come again." As there is no "maybe" in John 14:3, there is no "maybe" in James 5:15. Commentators agree that the sickness in James 5 is due to sin, even in light of the "if" in verse 15 (Mayor, p. 174; Ropes, pp. 308, 309; Tasker, p. 133; etc.).

The picture painted in this passage is of a man who has sinned and consequently is sick, flat on his back, at home, and unable to go and be reconciled to the one he has wronged. The word "sick" in verse 14 means "without strength." He cannot leave his sickbed, which is indicated by the fact that he is to call the elders to come to him rather than go to them.

The Procedure When a believer is sick because of his sin, so sick he is bedridden, he is to do three things. First, he is to call for the elders of the church who are to visit him in his home (or hospital room?). This passage does not describe a healing meeting but provides for a healing house call. The elders are to anoint the sick person with oil, which is symbolic, not medicinal. That is obvious from the fact that the prayer of faith saves the sick (Jas. 5:15), not the oil. The elders are also to pray for the sick saint.

As a result of the prayers of the elders, the Lord will "raise him up" (Jas. 5:15). Since sin caused his problem in the first place, and the sick person has acknowledged his sin by calling the elders, the ill believer can know the Lord will forgive him of his sin (Jas. 5:15). This does not necessarily mean that the Lord will completely heal him, at least not now. This is a two-stage healing. At this point, the sick man is "raised up," that is, he receives enough strength to do the next step. That must be the meaning of verse 15 because verse 16 instructs others to pray for his healing. So, the sick person is not completely healed at this point.

Second, the sick individual, now partially healed so that he has some of his strength back, is to confess his sin (Jas. 5:16). To whom is he to confess? Certainly not the Lord because the text says "to one another." Nor is it to the elders, for the phrase "one another" in Greek is a reciprocal pronoun meaning one another mutually. If this is a confession to the elders, the text demands that the elders confess their sins to the sick person!

Where is mutual confession appropriate? The answer is when two Christians have had a conflict and both have sinned. This supports the contention that the sickness in this passage was caused by sin. The sin was a conflict with another brother (Jas. 4:1-10). Both were guilty; both needed cleansing, and thus both needed confession.

Third, the sick person is to pray (Jas. 5:16). Again, this is mutual. The partially healed sick person and the reconciled brother are to pray for complete healing, which the Lord will do. James encourages them to pray by adding the story of Elijah (Jas. 5:16-18).

The point is God heals as a result of the prayers of elders when the sickness is because of sin. As A. C. Gaebelein says so well, "James 5:14 was never intended to be a remedy for all human ills in all cases, to be applied at all times in all places under all conditions" (Gaebelein, p. 79).

God Heals through Believers

What about sickness that is not the result of sin? Does God heal those kinds of illnesses and injuries? Is the only recourse of the believer to trust God to use doctors?

Does God heal today? The answer is "Yes." God wants believers to cast all of their care on Him (1 Pet. 5:7). Paul specifically says, "Be anxious for nothing, but in everything by prayer and supplication with thanksgiving, let your requests be made known unto God" (Phil. 4:6). In everything, God desires that we let our requests be made known, which includes asking God to heal. God "healed" Abimelech and his family in answer to prayer (Gen. 20:17-18).

God answers prayer. That includes prayer for healing. Throughout church history, believers have prayed, God has heard and answered, and as a result, sicknesses have been healed. The Swiss reformer Henry Bullinger, the successor to Zwingli, wrote, "Through confidence in the name of Christ, numbers greatly afflicted and shattered with disease are restored afresh to health." Richard Baxter declared that he knew of cases where "the prayer of faith to save the sick when all physicians had given them up as hopeless" succeeded. John Wesley, the founder of Methodism, related cases of answers to prayer in case of sickness.

Summary: God heals by means of doctors, the prayers of elders, and the prayers of believers.

When believers are sick, they should see a doctor and pray. Extremes should be avoided. Don't just see the doctor. Don't just pray. Do both. That is the biblical balance.

At the same time, believers should beware of the teaching that says: "Since all sickness is from Satan, and God wants all of His children well all of the time, and Christ died as a substitute for sickness, they can trust God and God will always heal them." That is simply not true. The Bible does not teach that; experience proves it does not work.

If it is not always God's will to heal, and Christ did not die for sickness as He did for sin, what is the basis of healing? John G. Mitchell says, "I believe it is a family matter. We come as children to a loving Father and make this request as we do any other. We come because of our relationship with Him. In John 16:23-28, six times in six verses our Lord talks about the Father.... He answers our request on the ground of His love. Now, as His children, we are in His love and care, in the care of one who has all authority in heaven and earth, and He looks down today and finds many of His children in suffering and affliction? Why should this be true? He always has a purpose and He always permits it because He loves us (Mitchell, pp. 51-52).

God loves you—so He may heal you.
God loves you—so He may not heal you because He has some other purpose in mind.

Chapter 8
CONCLUSION

Years ago, A. C. Gaebelein called the healing movement of his day, doctrinally the same as the one in our day, "One of the most subtle delusions of our time" (Gaebelein, p. 9). The healing movement is subtle. It sounds Scriptural, spiritual, and God-honoring. Verses ripped from their context appear to support its teaching.

A careful examination of the biblical data forces one to conclude that the healing theology of the modern American Protestant healing movement is healing heresy. It is a delusion. Not all sickness comes from Satan, nor is it the will of God for all to be healed. Jesus Christ did not die for sickness as He died for sin, and the Holy Spirit is not giving the gift of healing today. Some have had faith and were healed; others have had faith and were not. Faith is not the issue. Thus, the healing theology is heresy because it is not biblical.

Many of those teaching the healing heresy have been deceived and deluded. Some have been outright frauds and charlatans, like Marjoe Gortner. They all should have known better, not only from Scripture but from their own experience with sickness. Consider the following.

Dr. A. J. Gordon, the Boston Baptist who apparently was one of the first, if not the first, to suggest healing was in the atonement, fell victim to grippe, bronchitis, and pneumonia, sought a doctor, and took medicine. Dr. A. B. Simpson, who wrote *The Gospel of Healing* and founded the Christian and Missionary Alliance, was overcome by the hardening of the arteries and paralysis of the body and brain. In his declining years, he reluctantly used glasses. Concerning these two godly men and their ailments, Lockyer said, "When both Dr. Gordon and Dr. Simpson were ill, much prayer ascended on their behalf that God would grant them immediate and entire healing, but no deliverance came. God, in His inscrutable wisdom, withheld healing from His beloved servants, and both, in spite of prayer and faith and the ministry of physicians, nurses, and friends, died after a period of spiritual darkness in victory and praise" (Lockyer, p. 12).

That is only the beginning. It can get more sordid and morbid. Amy Simple MacPherson died in 1942, perhaps of suicide. A. A. Allen, who taught that God does not heal through medicine and went into scary details of what physicians do to patients, entered a hospital shortly before his death. He died of acute alcoholism and fatty inflammation of the liver in 1970. When his body was discovered, the police found several vials of pills in his possession (Simson, p. 111). In a Tulsa hospital on February 20, 1976, Kathryn Kuhlman died of a heart ailment she had had for years after she underwent open-heart surgery and was visited by Oral Roberts! (*Christianity Today*, Mar. 12, 1976, p. 47). Hobart Freeman was stricken with polio as a child and consequently walked with a pronounced limp until the day he died on December 8, 1984.

More tragic is the pain, sorrow, and death these deceived, influential leaders have caused their followers. Believers in healers

Conclusion

have been physically, emotionally, and spiritually hurt because of the teachings they have received and believed.

The healing heresy has caused physical harm. Countless thousands have suffered pain and agony because they were taught not to see a doctor. Many have been told they had been healed, but it had not been manifested yet. Deaths have been documented. The fact is that there are, no doubt, some psychosomatic cures that render the deliverance evangelist even more dangerous.

As Dr. Nolen stated, "Symptoms—pain, nausea, dizziness—may be purely psychological, but they may also be warning signs of dangerous possibly life-threatening organic (as opposed to functional) diseases. To eliminate a symptom without getting at the cause of that symptom can cause a delay in treatment, which may be serious or even fatal.... When healers treat serious organic diseases, they are responsible for untold anguish and unhappiness. This happens because they keep patients away from possibly effective and life-saving health. The healers become killers" (Nolen, p. 291,292).

The healing heresy has caused emotional harm. Packer points out, "To be told that longed-for healing was denied you because of some defect in your faith when you had labored and strained every way you knew to devote yourself to God and to "believe for blessing," is to be pitch-forked into distress, despair and a sense of abandonment by God. This is as bitter a feeling as any this side of hell--particularly if, like most invalids, your sensitivity is already up and your spirits down" (*Christianity Today*, May 21, 1982, p. 15).

Boggs said something similar. "It is difficult to exaggerate the spiritual agony and heartbreak that result. Case records of the way in which these healing failures are often followed by severe depression, obsession that the failure is due to a lack of faith, loss of religious faith by children, acute mania and other forms of insanity, and worsening of the physical affliction, are quoted by Gaebelein from the report of the investigation of the Price healing missions. Weatherford's testimony on this point is identical: 'It is no wonder that healing missions produce in many people black depression and hopeless despair. Most of those who attend them are not healed and their last state is often worse than their first'" (Boggs, p. 29).

A man named Mannie took his four-year-old daughter with an incurable malignant brain tumor to a supposedly Christian Filipino psychic surgeon and discovered they were all fakes. They said the problem for him was emotional: "I believed in them—the whole thing--and now I feel as if they were playing games with me. It hurts" (Nolen, p. 222).

The healing heresy has also caused untold spiritual damage. To be told that it is always God's will to heal and not be healed could drive the afflicted people to conclude that there are serious spiritual flaws in them. Either they are being punished for some sin or remain unhealed because of a lack of faith. It can and does get worse.

One Christian surgeon observed, "Many Christians who roll in wheelchairs, or awake each day to the scarred stumps of amputated limbs, or undergo the debility of spreading cancer have

Conclusion

prayed for healing. Some have attended healing services, felt the sudden rush of hope, and kneeled for the anointing of oil, yet still lived unhealed. For them, divine healing is the cruelest joke of all. At the precise moment when they most need support from the church, they receive instead an accusation that in spiritual, as well as in physical health, they do not measure up.

"Often on television or the radio, I hear speakers promise that healing is always available for all believers—a statement that approaches logical absurdity. If it were true, need any Christian wear glasses? ... In fact, in my own observation, an undue emphasis on divine healing causes far more sorrow than joy."

"Even worse, the habit of saying and praying what is unreal makes people begin to wonder if the whole of religion is unreal. If God does not "come through" in this manner of faith healing, when can He be counted on? Many people throw away their belief in a dependable God on account of their disillusionments over His lack of physical intervention" (*Christianity Today*, Nov. 25, 1983, p. 16).

When people who believe God is healing realize He is not, it's hard for them to remain a believer in anything Christian. The theology of the modern American Protestant healing movement is not only doctrinal heresy, but it is also downright harmful. The healing movement's teaching is (pardon the pun) unhealthy. At the end of a healing service, the doctor in search of a miracle observed,

"Finally, it was over. There were still long lines of people waiting to get on the stage and claim their cures, but the show ended at 5:00 with a hymn and a final blessing. Miss Kuhlman left the stage, and the audience left the auditorium. Before going back to Miss Kuhlman, I spent a few minutes watching the wheelchair patients leave. All the desperately ill patients who had been in wheelchairs were still in the wheelchairs. In fact, the man with the kidney cancer in his spine and hip, the man whom I'd helped to the auditorium and who had his borrowed wheelchair brought to the stage and shown to the audience when he had claimed a cure, was now back in his wheelchair. His 'cure,' even if only a hysterical one, had been extremely short-lived.

"As I stood in the corridor watching the hopeless cases leave, seeing the tears of the parents as they pushed their crippled children to the elevators, I wished Miss Kuhlman had been with me. She had complained a couple of times during the service of 'the responsibility, the enormous responsibility,' and of how her 'heart aches for those who weren't cured.' But I wondered how often she had really looked at them. I wondered whether she sincerely felt the joy of those 'cured' of bursitis and arthritis compensated for the anguish of those left with their withered legs, their imbecile children, their cancers of the liver. I wondered if she really knew what damage she was doing. I couldn't believe that she did" (Nolen, pp. 67-68).

BIBLIOGRAPHY

Angley, Ernest W. *Faith in God Heals the Sick.* Akron, Ohio: Winston Press, 1978.
Boggs, Wade H., Jr. *Faith Healing and the Christian Faith.* Richmond, Virginia: John Knox Press, 1956.
Bosworth, F. F. *Christ the Healer.* Old Tappan, New Jersey: Fleming H. Revell, 1973.
Brand, Paul and Yancy, Philip. "A Surgeon's View of Divine Healing I" *Christianity Today*, Nov. 25, '83, pp. 14-21.
Baxter, Richard. *The Practical Works of the Reverend Richard Baxter*, ed. William Orme, vol. 11, book 2, pp. 399-400.
Brand, Paul and Yancy, Philip. "A Surgeon's View of Divine Healing II." *Christianity Today*, Dec. 16, '83, pp. 12-17.
Burdick, Donald W. *Tongues: to Speak or Not to Speak.* Chicago: Moody press, 1972.
Calvin, John. *The Institutes of the Christian Religion.* Grand Rapids, Michigan: Associated Publishers and Authors, N.D.
Chafer, Lewis Sperry. *Systematic Theology*, III, Soteriology. Dallas, Texas: Dallas Seminary Press, 1948.
Copeland, Kenneth. *You Are Healed.* Fort Worth, Texas: KCP Publications, 1979.
Copeland, Kenneth. *God's Will Is Health* (tract). Fort Worth, Texas: Kenneth Copeland Ministries, N.D.
Copeland, Kenneth. *Our Covenant-Making God* (tract). Fort Worth, Texas: Kenneth Copeland Ministries, N.D.
Dart, John. "Skeptics' Revelations, Faith Healer Receives 'Heavenly' Messages Via Electronic Receiver." *Los Angeles Times*, May 11, '86, Part II section.
DeHaan, Dennis. "Running to Heaven." *Our Daily Bread.* Grand Rapids: Radio Bible Class, Sept. 4, 1981.

Freeman, Hobart E. *Faith*. Claypool, Indiana: Faith Publications, N.D.

Gaebelein, Arno Clemens. *The Healing Question*. New York, New York: "Our Hope" Publication Office, N.D.

Godet, Frederick Louis. *Commentary on the Gospel of John*, Vol. II. Grand Rapids, Michigan: Zondervan Publishing House, 1893 (reprint).

Gordon, A.J. *Ministry of Healing*. Boston, Mass.: Howard Gannett, 1882.

Hagin, Kenneth E. *Seven Things You Should Know About Divine Healing*. Tulsa, Oklahoma: Kenneth Hagin Ministries, 1979.

Hagin, Kenneth E. *The Name of Jesus*. Tulsa, Oklahoma: Kenneth Hagin Ministries, 1979.

Harrell, David Edwin, Jr. *All Things Are Possible*. Bloomington, Indiana: Indiana University Press, 1975.

Hiebert, D. Edmond. *Second Timothy*. Chicago, Illinois: Moody Press, 1958.

Hodge, Charles. *A Commentary on the Second Epistle to the Corinthians*. London: The Banner of Truth Trust, 1963.

Hoekema, Anthony A. *What About Tongue-Speaking?* Grand Rapids, Michigan: Wm. B. Eerdmans, 1966.

Keil, C. F. *The Books of the Chronicles*, trans. Andrew Harper. Grand Rapids, Michigan: Wm. B. Eerdmans, 1968.

Kent, Homer A., Jr. *The Pastoral Epistles, Studies in I and II Timothy and Titus*. Chicago, Illinois: Moody Press, 1958.

Lindsay, Gordon. *John Alexander Dowie*. Dallas, Texas: Christ for the Nations, reprint 1980.

Lenski, R. C. H. *The Interpretation of St. Paul's First and Second Epistles to the Corinthians*. Minneapolis, Minn.: Augsburg Publishing House, 1963.

Lightner, Robert P. *Speaking in Tongues and Divine Healing*. Schaumburg, Illinois: Regular Baptist Press, 1978.

Lockyer, Herbert. *Is There Healing for All?* Oklahoma City, Oklahoma: The Western Network Radio Church of the Air, N.D.
MacArthur, John, Jr. *The Charismatics*. Grand Rapids, Michigan: Zondervan, 1978.
Mayhue, Richard. *Divine Healing Today*. Chicago, Illinois: Moody Press, 1983.
Mayor, Joseph B. *The Epistle of St. James*. Grand Rapids, Michigan: Zondervan, 1913 (reprint 1954).
McClain, Alva J. *Was Christ Punished for Our Diseases?* Winona Lake, Indiana: The Brethren Missionary Herald, N.D.
Mitchell, John G. "Does God Heal Today?" *Bibliotheca Sacra*, Jan-Mar, '65, Vol. 122, No. 485. Dallas, Texas: Dallas Seminary Press, pp. 41-53.
Morris, Leon. *The Gospel of John*. Grand Rapids, Michigan: Wm. B. Eerdmans, 1971.
Nolen, William A. *Healing: A Doctor in Search of a Miracle*. New York: Random House, 1974.
Orme, William, ed. *The Practical Works of the Reverend Richard Baxter*, Vol. 11, Bk. 2. London: James Duncan, 1830.
Packer, James I. "Poor Health May Be the Best Remedy." *Christianity Today*, May 21, 1982, pp. 14-16.
Peters, George W. *Indonesia Revival, Focus on Timor*. Grand Rapids, Michigan: Zondervan, 1974.
Randi, James, et. al. "Faith-Healing, Miracle or Fraud?" *Free Inquiry*, Spring '86, vol. 6, No. 2.
Roberts, Oral. *God Still Heals Today and Here's How He Heals You*. Tulsa, Oklahoma: Oral Roberts, 1984.
_____. *If You Need Healing—Do These Things*. Tulsa, Oklahoma: Standard Printing Co., 1947.
_____. *Master Key to Healing*. Tulsa, Oklahoma: Standard Printing Co., 1959.

Ropes, James Hardy. *A Critical and Exegetical Commentary on the Epistle of St. James.* Edinburgh: T. & T. Clark, 1916 (reprint 1954).

Simson, Eve. *The Faith Healer.* St. Louis, Missouri: Concordia, 1977.

Spurgeon, C. H. *Spurgeon's Popular Exposition of Matthew.* Grand Rapids, Michigan: Zondervan, 1893 (reprint 1962).

Stafford, Tim. "Testing the Wine from John Wimber's Vineyard." *Christianity Today*, Aug. 8, '86, pp. 17-22.

Tasker, R. V. G. *The General Epistle of James.* Grand Rapids, Michigan: Wm. B. Eerdmans, 1960.

Westcott, Brooke Foss. *The Epistle to the Hebrews.* Grand Rapids, Michigan: Wm. B. Eerdmans, 1889.

Wuest, Kenneth S. *Wuest's Word Studies from the Greek New Testament*, Vol. 2, Philippians—Hebrews, The Pastoral Epistles—First Peter. Grand Rapids, Michigan: Wm. B. Eerdmans, 1966.

Yancey, Philip, *Where Is God When It Hurts?* Grand Rapids, Michigan: Zondervan, 1978.

About The Author

G. Michael Cocoris is a gifted communicator. He can make even complicated subjects simple, clear, and practical. His breadth of experience has allowed him to relate to a wide range of audiences.

Michael received a Bachelor of Arts degree from Tennessee Temple University, a Master of Theology degree from Dallas Seminary, and a Doctorate of Divinity from Biola University. He traveled the United States for over a dozen years as a speaker. He has also been a seminary professor, visiting lecturer, and world traveler, including hosting tours to Israel and China.

Michael has pastored three churches, including a rural church when he was in seminary, an urban church, the historic Church of the Open Door, first in downtown Los Angeles and later in Glendora, California, and a suburban church, the Lindley Church in Tarzana California, a suburb of Los Angeles. While at the Church of Open Door, he had a daily radio broadcast.

Michael has written numerous magazine articles, mainly for *Biblical Research Monthly*. He has authored a number of books, including *Seventy Years on Hope Street, A History of the Church of the Open Door*; *The Spiritual Life, Clarifying the Confusion; Repentance, The Most Misunderstood Word in the Bible; Evangelism: A Biblical Approach; The Salvation Controversy; Lordship Salvation: Is It Biblical?; The Books of the Bible, the Subject, Structure, Situation, and Significant Verses of Each Book; Psalms, A Song for Every Situation, Each Summarized on One Page; and Counseling Theories: A Simple Explanation and Biblical Evaluation*. In addition, he was a contributor to The *NKJV Study Bible* and *Nelson's New Illustrated Bible Commentary*.

Michael is the pastor of the Lindley Church in Tarzana, California. He and his wife, Patricia, live in Santa Monica, California.

www.ingramcontent.com/pod-product-compliance
Lightning Source LLC
Chambersburg PA
CBHW070114080526
44586CB00013B/1289